Joseph Frederick Dripps

A Sketch of the Work and Worship of the First Presbyterian Church in Germantown

Joseph Frederick Dripps

A Sketch of the Work and Worship of the First Presbyterian Church in Germantown

ISBN/EAN: 9783337293178

Printed in Europe, USA, Canada, Australia, Japan

Cover: Foto ©Lupo / pixelio.de

More available books at **www.hansebooks.com**

FIRST PRESBYTERIAN CHURCH, GERMANTOWN.

A SKETCH

OF

THE WORK AND WORSHIP

OF THE

𝕱𝖎𝖗𝖘𝖙 𝕻𝖗𝖊𝖘𝖇𝖞𝖙𝖊𝖗𝖎𝖆𝖓 𝕮𝖍𝖚𝖗𝖈𝖍

IN

GERMANTOWN.

PREPARED BY
REV. J. F.ᴸ DRIPPS,
PASTOR, 1870-1880.

PUBLISHED BY THE SESSION.
1880.

GRANT, FAIRES & RODGERS,
PRINTERS,
54 NORTH SIXTH STREET,
PHILADELPHIA.

Church Officers, etc.

———— • ————

PASTOR.

Rev. J. FREDERIC DRIPPS.

SESSION.

The Pastor, ex-officio Moderator, with Ruling Elders:

T. CHARLTON HENRY,	CHARLES M. LUKENS,
THOMAS MACKELLAR,	ENOCH TAYLOR,
EDWARD L. WILSON.	

BOARD OF TRUSTEES.

EDWARD COPE,	SAMUEL G. DENNISON,
JOHN GARRETT,	JONATHAN GRAHAM,
J. BAYARD HENRY,	THOMAS F. JONES,
JAMES KINNIER,	THOMAS MACKELLAR,
CHARLTON H. ROYAL,	ENOCH TAYLOR.

SABBATH-SCHOOL SUPERINTENDENTS.

Home School, - - T. CHARLTON HENRY.

Pulaskiville School, - ISAAC C. JONES, Jr.

Somerville School, - GEORGE F. WIGGAN.

MISSIONARIES.

Chapel Minister, - Rev. JAMES W. KIRK.

Bible-Reader, - - Mrs. C. D. SCOTT.

Foreign Missionary, - Mrs. JOHN C. BALLAGH.

PASTORAL AID SOCIETY.

President, - - Mrs. MARY D. WESTCOTT.

Secretary, - - Miss JEANNIE H. BACON.

Treasurer, - - Mrs. THOMAS F. JONES.

EXECUTIVE COMMITTEE.

Mrs. WESTCOTT and Miss BACON, Ex-officio.

Mrs. J. F. DRIPPS, Mrs. T. CHARLTON HENRY,

Mrs. JONATHAN GRAHAM.

YOUNG MEN'S SOCIETY.

President, - - J. ADDISON CAMPBELL.

Secretary, - - HARRY K. MANSFIELD

Treasurer, - - GEORGE Q. SPIEGEL.

PREFACE.

Ten years have elapsed since the present pastor began work in this church. Its record during that time includes the following facts, which are here brought together for more convenient reference, in the form of a brief summary.

The number of persons who have been received into Communion is 348; of whom, 220 came upon profession of faith. Two of these members have been ordained to the Gospel ministry. There are at the present time 372 names on the roll.

A new church has been erected; the building and furniture costing $70,296.00. Of this sum, $21,564.00 came from the sale of the old church, and the remainder, $48,732.00 was paid in cash.

Two mission stations have been formed, and a chapel built for each. In the Sunday-Schools which are held in these chapels, together with that which meets in the church itself, there is a total enrolled membership of 901. On the Somerville field there is a Chapel Minister, giving his whole time to the work, and holding three services weekly. In other directions an efficient Bible-reader has been steadily engaged, with most encouraging results. The ladies have been organized into a Pastoral Aid Society, which has at present sixteen Standing Committees, each with its own distinct form of effort, in the congregation, the neighborhood, or the mission field. It supports a Missionary in Japan, and maintains scholarships there and elsewhere. There are 75 members in the Society, and it has received contributions amounting, by the end of 1879, to about $30,000.00.

The gifts of the church during this decade, for all such purposes, religious and benevolent, have been considerably more than $175,000.00.

As the Seventieth anniversary of the church occurs within the year, it has been thought best to sketch its earlier history also; incorporating with this, the facts which were partially recorded in the Manual printed eight years ago.

7

THE

FIRST PRESBYTERIAN CHURCH

IN

GERMANTOWN.

THERE is but little in the present appearance of this church to show that it originated from German stock, and was for many years entitled, "The English Church in Germantown." Yet such a fact cannot have been without influence on its history and life. There surely is such a thing as continuous life and individual character in a church; and its work and worship can best be carried on by those who know that history, and so enter with sympathy and intelligence into their places in its life. It is worth while to trace backward this particular record, if only to perceive more clearly that the sincere purpose of obeying God, and serving the gospel of His Son, was the controlling motive which led to the foundation, not only of the edifice in which we meet, and of that which preceded it, but of the church itself, and of the church from which it grew, and even of the very town in which they were established.

GERMANTOWN, or THE GERMAN TOWNSHIP, as it is called in some of the older records, was from its very foundation distinctly religious. It was "freedom to worship God" which its German settlers were seeking when they left their home in the Palatinate. The first arrivals reached here in 1683, a few months after the settlement of Philadelphia, and for more than fifty years increasing numbers joined them, impelled by the same willingness to live as exiles in the American wilderness, rather than give up religious freedom. The armies of Roman Catholic France depopulated many a Protestant German village, only to send its inhabitants westward to Pennsylvania. So great were the numbers of these exiles, that the authorities of this Province seem to have been more than once not a little alarmed lest Pennsylvania should become German, and not English; and the population of the State has always consisted of this stock in far greater proportion than is generally known. So late as 1751, nearly one-half of all its inhabitants were German. Most of these settlements, however, were in other parts of the Province; there was but one German town in the immediate neighborhood of Philadelphia. Some of its first settlers had, before crossing the ocean, joined the "Society of Friends," which had but recently been organized, and whose originator, Fox, was still living. Others of them took the same step after reaching this country, so that the house which Pastorius, the leader in this immigration, erected as a place of worship in 1686, was at once used by this Society for its meetings. Such meetings had already been held in a private house since 1683.

This was the first religious organization in Germantown, and Pastorius himself became one of its leading members. He was a highly educated man, and seems to have kept its records in the English language from the beginning, though German was spoken at the meetings.

The first public testimony which was ever given against Slavery, came from this meeting in 1688: though the

German Friends did not find their appeal seconded by their English neighbors, who were not as yet in advance of their fellow-countrymen in this matter.

In 1708 the Mennonists of Germantown formed a church of fifty-two members, and in 1723 the Tunkers or Dunkards organized one in the district named after one of the settlers, Bebberstown, since corrupted to Beggarstown.

The next church was that from which our own is descended. There were, by this time quite a large number of the German Reformed in this country: in 1731 they were estimated at 15,000. But there was an utter absence as yet of regular pastors; the home church in Germany was so persecuted and down-trodden that it could not supply its own wants, much less those of the exiles in America. The Reformed Church of Holland was appealed to, and for many years all work among the Germans here was fostered by the Dutch Classis of Amsterdam.

The first efforts in this direction came, however, in very unpretending shape, from among the colonists themselves; men of earnest christian hearts, moved by the spiritual needs around them, exerted themselves to do what they could, and ultimately found themselves called by the people, and ordained by the church authorities, as ministers of the gospel.

Such a man was the founder of this particular church in Germantown, the Rev. John Bechtel. His writings and his life itself show him to be a warm-hearted christian of the true apostolic spirit. When he reached this country in 1726, being at the time 38 years old, he began immediate efforts for the spiritual welfare of his fellow colonists.

Acting simply as a layman, he held religious meetings for his neighbors at his own house, and this not on

Sundays alone, but twice each day through the week.   In a letter written by him afterward in 1744, he declares that "for the last sixteen years, (that is, since 1728, two years after his arrival) I have served the Reformed brethren as preacher, according to a call from them, and a written confirmation of it from Heidelberg in Germany." He was not formally ordained until 1742, when Bishop Nitschman of the Moravian Church took the chief part in the service.   Long before this, however, in 1733, five years after his call and licensure to preach, his people erected the first German Reformed Church Building in the State, and Divine Worship was regularly conducted in it thenceforward.   The pastors who succeeded him, were no less consecrated and fervent, and they were men of highly educated minds, regularly trained for the ministry, and coming to this country in the veritable missionary spirit. One of them especially, Rev. Michael Schlatter, was widely honored throughout the Province for his character and work by all classes and churches.   He was, to this church, what his friend Muhlenberg was to the Lutheran body.

It was not until two generations of church life had thus passed away, that the events took place which resulted in the formation of our own church.   From 1805 to 1811, the Reformed Congregation had no settled pastor.   So severely was this destitution felt, that in 1807 the congregation at Frankford, which was a branch of this one in Germantown and under its care, transferred itself to the Presbytery of Philadelphia, and has since that time always had English-speaking Presbyterian pastors.   This action was taken unanimously; and the people assigned as their reasons, that they could in no other way maintain religious services at all, and that they considered the shades of difference between the German Reformed Church and the

Presbyterian Church to be very slight. The lines of distinction between denominations were less firmly drawn than now. The desire for service in the English language had much influence with the congregation, as indeed it had with all the other German churches of the city at that time. Each of them came to a point at which the younger members, who spoke only English, either changed the worship of their church into that language, or, as was usually the case, found themselves obliged to form a new church. The need was as pressing in Germantown as elsewhere. Indeed, Rev. Mr. Runkel, who resigned in 1805, had been in the habit of preaching in both languages alternately. His preaching at Frankfort was in English three times out of four. And even after his departure, the Germantown church is known to have had many English services. But the older members finally refused to continue this compromise, and voted to call a pastor from Germany, who should use only his native language in all his preaching. Of those who then formed the younger generation in the church, several are yet living; and they attest the fact that German services were wholly unintelligible to a large proportion among the youth of their day. The attachment of the older members for their native language is easily understood; yet the change was inevitable sooner or later, and for men who had permanently identified themselves with an English-speaking nation, it was really as desirable as necessary. The younger members began to feel that there was no alternative but to organize a church whose worship they could understand.

This step was the more natural because of the example which had already been given in this city, and by the Frankford branch of this church itself.

Mr. Joseph Miller, one of the leading members of the

congregation, was a chief mover in the new enterprise. The following information concerning him is given in a letter from his grandson, Franklin B. Gowen, Esq. :

" Mr. Joseph Miller, my maternal grandfather, was born at Mount Airy, (in the upper part of Germantown) on January 16th, 1757, and died at Mount Airy March 27th, 1825. He married Susanna Raser, who was born January 12, 1767, and who long survived him, dying in Philadelphia, September 23d, 1853. In 1792 he built the stone house at Mount Airy, in which he subsequently lived and died, in which my mother and myself were born, in which I recently lived, and which is now occupied by my brother, Mr. James E. Gowen."

His father, Sebastian Miller, or, as he invariably wrote his name, "Sebastian Müller," was undoubtedly German : his marriage is on record as taking place in Germantown, April 10th, 1754. The family was one of the oldest in connection with the German Reformed Congregation, and Mr. Joseph Miller was a prominent man in the community. It was with great reluctance that he left the old church, and his whole life and character confirms the declaration, that he really felt himself compelled by the religious necessities of his own children, and of the youth around him, to act as a chief founder of the new organization.

Another prominent figure in the little company was that of the Rev. Samuel Blair, D. D., son of the well-known Presbyterian minister of that name. He was therefore of Scotch-Irish descent, and was born in Chester County, Pennsylvania, in 1741. When but twenty-six years old, he had been elected to the Presidency of Princeton College, but on finding that Dr. Witherspoon could be induced to cross the ocean and accept the position, he resigned in his favor. After spending three years in Boston, as colleague with Dr. Sewall, in the Old South Church, he came in 1769 to Germantown, where he lived in retirement, possessed of a comfortable estate, and engaged chiefly in literary pursuits, until his death in 1818.

In some respects the times were not propitious for such an undertaking, as that of which we are now speaking; for the events which culminated in the war of 1812 were already producing great disturbance in commercial and social relations. Indeed, one of the earliest services held in the new edifice after it was at last completed, was for the benefit of a military company enlisted for the war. The occasion is well remembered by some who were present.

Yet in other respects, it was a season decidedly favorable to religious activity. There was everywhere a reaction from the spiritual depression which had been felt during the generation immediately following the Revolutionary War. The Foreign Missionary work in this country, the Sunday School Union, the Theological Seminary at Princeton, were all lifted into existence at the same time with this little church, and by the same rising tide of spiritual influence. Our Presbyterian Home Mission work had but just been fully organized; there had been great revivals in the land, such as had not been vouchsafed for more than one generation. All such events are surely connected one with another, not always by any conscious purpose of men, but by the purpose and intention of that One Person, that Holy Spirit, who fills every member and part of Christ's Body, the Church. There was, by His grace, a great spring-tide of religious life throughout the whole church in this country; and there is a new interest in looking at God's Providential dealings with this humble German village, when we conceive of them as forming one manifestation of that water of life which was flooding all the coasts of our land.

It was held to be Providential indeed, by the Germantown people, that just at this time there came into the
village the Rev. Thomas Dunn, who in due time became
the first pastor of our church. This might have been less
remarkable, if he had come in the character of a minister
seeking a church, or sought by one : but the circumstances
were not of this kind. He was born in Devonshire,
England, in 1763, and educated in the Baptist Church at
Bristol, under the charge of Dr. Evards and the celebrated
Robert Hall. He received pressing calls from different
churches in England, which are still in possession of his
family. By the advice of Lord Erskine he left England in
1793, on account of the opposition which had been excited
by his publishing a pamphlet, which was too democratic
for the times. He preached for some time in Philadelphia
and in Newport, but on account of ill-health exchanged
this for a business life. It was not, therefore, as a minister,
but as a layman, doing occasionally ministerial work, that
he removed to Germantown, which he did in 1809. He
had not given up his interest in gospel work, however, and
finding the spiritual need of the community to be very
pressing, he at once entered with great heartiness into the
effort of supplying it.

The Reformed Congregation invited him to conduct
services for them ; there being, as already stated, no pastor
at the time. He accepted this invitation immediately, and
there was for a time some prospect of his becoming himself
the pastor, in which case the new church would not have
been required. He had some time previously changed his
views concerning Baptism, and become Presbyterian on
conviction, and now, in October 1809, he applied for
reception under care of the Presbytery of Philadelphia, as
a licensed preacher. There was considerable delay, however, from various causes, in perfecting these arrangements.

The fact that Mr. Dunn had come from another country, as well as from another denomination, made it necessary, according to the constitution of our church, that at least one year should intervene before his final reception into this body. At the end of the year, however, in October 1810, he was formally received under care of Presbytery. It was then agreed by Presbytery that since Mr. Dunn had "for more than a year been preaching to a congregation within our bounds, to the satisfaction of the people," he should be regularly appointed to preach for the new church. It was not yet a church, entirely organized as such; and this fact made fresh delay. The Presbytery commissioned Dr. Archibald Alexander to visit Germantown and explain to the people that until their organization was more complete, so that a regular "call" could be extended by them to Mr. Dunn, the way would not be open for his ordination. They did indeed form a distinct congregation; for it had some time previously become evident that the authorities of the German Reformed Congregation would not consent to any further English services; and those persons who felt the need of such services had withdrawn with the intention of constituting an English Church. For about two years they continued to meet in the house of Dr. Blair, a commodious building, which is still standing on the eastern corner of the Main street and Walnut Lane: the same building which was in after years occupied for awhile, by the "Manual Labor Academy," an institution which developed into Lafayette College, on its removal to Easton. It was always their purpose, however, to erect a new edifice as soon as possible, and by March 1811, the first subscription books were opened. In the heading of these books it is specified that the building was to be "for the use of a Christian society, formed on the principles and rules of the Presbyterian Church, under the superintendency of the

General Assembly of said Church in the United States."
While this work of preparation was going on, Mr. Dunn
received ordination, June 19, 1811; the Presbytery of
Philadelphia meeting for that purpose in the Methodist
Church of Germantown. Dr. Archibald Alexander presided, Rev. Nathaniel Irwin preached, and Dr. Ashbel
Green delivered the charge. It had been intended to
confer this ordination the previous year, but some technical
difficulties prevented.

The site for the building was then chosen, and an
agreement made with its owner, John Detweiler, for
eight hundred pounds. At the same meeting a Building
Committee was appointed, consisting of Joseph Miller,
Henry Bruner, Joseph Jacobs, William Sinclair, Robert
Bringhurst, William Stewart, Jr., Jacob Miller and George
I. Howell; Joseph Miller being Treasurer and Isaac
Robardeau Secretary. July 30, the building was staked
off; August 5, ground was broken; August 21, the deeds
were finally signed by Mr. Detweiler and wife, after the
reluctance of the latter had been overcome by giving her
fifty dollars extra for signing, and promising her one
hundred cabbages to replace the set vegetables then
growing in the garden. The details of all these trans-
actions are recorded with great minuteness by Mr.
Robardeau. Sept. 10, the corner-stone was laid, Dr.
Blair presiding, and Rev. Mr. Dunn making the address.
In January, 1812, an effort was made, which was repeated
in 1815, to procure legislative sanction for the holding of
a lottery to raise $12,000; but this project, which was
in those days quite as ordinary as church fairs are now,
was never carried into effect. In February, 1812, the
committee, "under a due sense of the benevolent labors
of Mr. Dunn," rented him a parsonage, paying for it by
subscription.

The record closes thus: "Resolved, That the committee, sensible of the obligations which they, in common with their fellow citizens in the vicinity, are under to Mr. Dunn for his disinterested and affectionate attentions, direct that this testimony of their gratitude and disposition to reward his services be entered on the Records of the Church, at the same time regretting that, from the present situation of the institution, it is out of their power to offer him suitable compensation."

In April, Presbytery commended this church to the city congregations for aid, on the suggestion of Dr. Blair.

On Sabbath, July 19, 1812, the church building was dedicated to God, Mr. Dunn holding the dedicatory services at 11 A. M., and Dr. Alexander preaching at 4 P. M.

It was forty-five feet wide, sixty-five feet deep, and the ceiling had a height of thirty feet at the cornice and thirty-three feet at the apex. It cost $17,000, (part of which was still unpaid, however) and was a substantial and creditable structure.

During the same month an agreement was made by Dr. Blair and Mr. Joseph Miller for an organ of fourteen stops, costing $1200, to be finished within one year by Alexander Schlotman. Mr. Miller added to his other useful offices, that of organist for many years. August 30, the first communion service was held in the new church. twenty-seven communicants partaking.

October 26, Joseph Miller, Samuel Blair, Henry Bruner and William Turnbull were ordained to the eldership. In March, 1813, a Board of Deacons was ordained. On the second Thursday in May, Mr. Dunn was finally installed as Pastor, Rev. Messrs. Potts, Latta and Doake taking part in the service. Mr. Dunn's salary was $800. In June additional elders and deacons were ordained. In April, 1814, the first election under the charter was held.

This charter provided for giving the care of temporal affairs to a "Vestry" consisting of twenty-six members, serving for four years. The elders were permanent members *ex officio:* the others were divided into four classes, and one class was elected each year. Dr. Blair was the first president of this Vestry; Joseph Miller treasurer and John Cameron secretary. In June, 1814, it is recorded that on account of Mr. Dunn's ill health, the afternoon service was omitted and the evening service continued, which indicates that three services had been held previously. This is one among many indications of Mr. Dunn's energy and faithfulness.

In October, 1815, Mr. Dunn resigned his charge on account of ill health, which prevented his maintaining such active work.

He had been preaching continuously to this people, since the summer of 1809; in the German Reformed edifice at first, then at Dr. Blair's and in the new church. When he began this work, he was some forty-seven years of age, and known as an able and attractive preacher. Contemporary records show that he produced a decided impression for good upon the community at large; and on the part of the congregation it is said that "God has sent unto us in a very remarkable manner a preacher eminently qualified for this glorious work, in whom all are united, and whose ministry has hitherto been greatly blessed." He afterward resided chiefly at Newport, R. I., until his death in 1833; and we are glad to know that the same qualities which enabled him to be of so inestimable benefit to the church in this place have in his descendants produced similar results elsewhere. His grandson, Rev. Robinson Potter Dunn, D. D., was well known as pastor of the First Presbyterian Church of Camden, New Jersey, and Professor in Brown University: he also received a call to the pastorate of this church in subsequent years. We regret that the limits of this sketch prevent our dwelling at length upon his noble character and work, or that of the pastors who succeeded him.

Before the end of November, 1815, Session and Vestry made an agreement with Rev. George Bourne, member of the Presbytery of Lexington, in Virginia, to supply the pulpit for a year ; two services to be held on Sabbath and one on Thursday evening : salary, $600. Mr. Bourne informed the Session that action had been taken against him by the Presbytery of Lexington, chiefly on account of his bold denunciation of slavery ; but it refused to give any weight to these charges, and in January, 1816, he began regular service in Germantown.

In March, the Presbytery of Philadelphia notified the church that this action was deemed irregular, whereupon the people warmly sustained Mr. Bourne : indeed, they carried it so far that Dr. Blair resigned his seat in Presbytery and the church withdrew from connection with it. On June 16, Mr. Bourne was formally elected pastor of the church.

In March, 1817, we find the church settling some difficulties which had arisen among the people in consequence of this ecclesiastical position, by calling upon Rev. Messrs. Ely, Staughton, Wilson, Parker and Patterson to act as an advisory council.

In May, the General Assembly referred back Mr. Bourne's case to the Presbytery of Lexington, on account of the insufficiency of proof against him and the over-severity of his sentence.

In October, Dr. Blair resumed his seat as a member of the Presbytery of Philadelphia, Dr. William Neill and Mr. Dunn having conferred with him on behalf of that body.

In January, 1818, steps were taken by the church vestry towards re-uniting with the Presbytery; and on March 29th, at a church meeting moderated by Dr. Ely, a letter was addressed to it requesting to be considered as again one of its constituents, and asking it to sanction Mr. Bourne's officiating as stated minister for the present. On April 21, the Presbytery did accordingly receive the church again into membership.

In May, however, the General Assembly of the year decided against Mr. Bourne. This occasioned a division of sentiment among the congregation; but as the officers took decided action in support of the General Assembly's authority, Mr. Bourne withdrew in June, with the purpose of forming a new organization. On July 14th, we find the Presbytery, on application of the elders from this church, appointing supplies for the pulpit. July 27, the vestry appointed a committee to choose arbitrators between Mr. Bourne and the church. On September 13th, Mr. Bourne organized the " Shiloh Independent Church " in Germantown, with thirty members. It continued in existence only a few months, however.

Mr. Bourne was of English birth, and was licensed in London, A. D. 1804. The next ten years of his life were spent in Virginia and Maryland. After leaving Germantown, he took charge of an academy at Sing Sing and supplied the Presbyterian pulpit. He was afterward pastor of the Congregational Church at Quebec; then at New York City, and at West Farms, in Reformed Dutch churches. He died in 1845, aged sixty-five. He was a man of considerable literary attainments as well as personal piety; and his power is sufficiently shown by his fearless attacks upon slavery in Virginia and upon popery in Quebec. It is gratifying to know that he survived these troublous experiences at Germantown for nearly thirty years, and continued in the work of the ministry up to old age with so great power and usefulness. The church roll showed twenty-nine members at his accession : he added forty to the list, and has left on record thirty-six baptisms. In October, 1818, Dr. William Neill and Rev. Mr. Potts were appointed a committee to visit and counsel the Germantown Church on behalf of Presbytery; and in December, Dr. Neill introduced to that body Rev. James Rooker, with the view of having him recognized as pastor of this church. Mr. Rooker was accordingly accepted as a licentiate, (December 17,) with expressions of high regard for himself and appreciation of his previous usefulness as an Independent. He, like both of his predecessors, was of English birth, and was at this time sixty-two years of age ; but although a man of great experience and worth, seems to have had no ordination until June, 1819, when he was ordained and installed as pastor of this church. Dr. Neill presided ; Rev. Thomas H. Skinner preached the sermon, and Rev. J. K. Burch gave the charges.

April 25, 1819, "a Sunday School was opened in the church for instructing the children to read and learn by heart portions of Scripture." By a record in 1825, we find that the church was in the habit of regular contributions to the " United Foreign Missionary Society," by collections taken at the monthly concerts. April 20th, 1826, Mr. Rooker resigned his pastoral charge from infirm health and advanced age, though he continued to administer the ordinances until his death in December, 1828, at the age of seventy-three. The church records show that he found thirty-one members enrolled at his accession; he added fifty-six, and performed seventy-four baptisms. He is remembered, however, less by such details of work than by the deep impression made by his beautiful christian character. In the interval which followed his resignation, there occurred another crisis in the church history.

In April, 1827, there being some $3000 debt on the
church, the property was deeded over to Rev. Drs. E. S.
Ely and J. J. Janeway, of the Presbytery of Philadelphia,
on condition of their assuming this debt; and for about
five years the title to the property was in their hands.
On Mr. Rooker's death, Rev. James Nourse supplied the
pulpit during 1829 and part of 1830, adding eight to the
roll. After several other brethren had taken charge for
shorter periods, Rev. Dr. George Junkin preached for
several months, adding twenty-two to the roll of members.
He was then principal of the "Manual Labor Academy"
in Germantown, and is said in his biography to have found
here "a good church building, with the nucleus of a congregation."

In September, 1831, Dr. William Neill, who had long
been familiarly acquainted with the church, assumed personal charge of it, remaining in this connection until
September, 1842. With Dr. Neill in regular charge, the
condition of affairs began to improve, and the congregation
prepared to resume control of their property.

It seemed desirable, however, to make several changes
in the constitution of the church; and, to accomplish this,
the members of the "English Presbyterian Church" caused
themselves to be organized by Legislative act (June 12,
1832) into a new corporation, with a new title, viz.: "The
First Presbyterian Church in Germantown." There has
been no serious incumbrance on the property since the
church has borne the present title. Several small claims
did remain unsatisfied for some years; but on August 21,
1836, it is recorded as "being free from all debt whatever."

It was by no means strong in its number of members,
however, for a long time after this.

During Dr. Neill's connection with the church, we find
Mr. William D. Howard (afterward the Rev. Dr. Howard

of Pittsburgh) serving as elder, and as President of the Board of Trustees, 1835–38.

In 1838, the use of the church building on Sabbath afternoons and evenings was given to the German Reformed church pending the completion of their new edifice.

In August, 1841, a congregational library was established by Dr. Neill.

In September of 1842, he resigned his position, and passed his declining years in retirement, at his home in Philadelphia. He is well-known throughout the entire church from the prominent positions he held as Stated Clerk of General Assembly, &c. He had already filled a long life with good deeds when he came to Germantown, and his residence here is still remembered with great interest. He admitted forty-three members, and performed fifty-eight baptisms.

From September, 1842, until April, 1850, Rev. Thomas B. Bradford had charge of the church. He found fifty-three enrolled members; added one hundred and twenty-five, and performed sixty-five baptisms. There is little of strongly-marked incident recorded of these years, but they have had a decided influence for good on the character of the church; its whole spirit became more hopeful and aggressive. He resigned his charge in 1850, on account of painful bodily ailments; and was never able to resume pastoral work, although rendering considerable services to weak churches in his own vicinity, until his death, in 1871, after a long and painful illness.

From October, 1850, until June, 1852, Rev. Septimus Tustin, D. D., performed a good work in this congregation. Fifty-six were added to its membership, and the tide of prosperity was rising steadily, when he felt himself called in another direction, and was dismissed by the church with great reluctance. He also is widely known throughout the church as pastor of several important congregations, chaplain for many years in Congress, and especially as delegate from the Old School General Assembly to that of the New School, in 1863, inaugurating the Re-union movement. Dr. Tustin died in September, 1871; so that of all the pastors up to this year (1852) not one remains yet alive.

They deserve much larger notice than it is possible to give them within these brief pages. We are thankful to know that they are not dependent for reward or appreciation upon us: that there is a record on high, wherein is no omission, a Master who is not unjust to forget their "work and labor of love." Theirs is the fame which is not confined to earth, where it can only sound over their unhearing bodies; but that which comes to their glorified spirits, from the souls whom they led after them to heaven, and from the blessed angels, and from that King whose generous praise is given to every good and faithful servant. Not because they need it, but for our own sakes, do we call to mind their work in the cause of this church; so patient and persevering through trials and difficulties which we know to have been neither few nor small. The high regard in which they were held by the community at large, as men who were, on the whole, of decidedly more than usual ability, and of true devotion and earnestness, was itself no small help to the church.

It needs to be remembered that the field in which they labored bears a very different aspect in our day from that which it then presented. Instead of being a lovely but somewhat remote country village, inhabited largely by men speaking a foreign tongue, Germantown has become an integral part of Philadelphia itself. It was always attractive and comparatively populous. Before the Revolution, it is said to have had "more houses and people than any other town in the Province, except Philadelphia and

Lancaster." There were hardly more than 2000 inhabitants, however, when this church was organized; in 1830 it claimed to have 4000. The growth in later years was far more rapid.

The change from its foreign aspect was very gradual. In 1709, the English Government refused to continne its land-owners in possession of their land, unless they became naturalized; but in speech and habits they were found to be still German, even in 1793, when the National Government, with Washington at is head, came to Germantown for a time, to escape the yellow fever in Philadelphia. From that time onward, however, so many English-speaking residents came in, that the inevitable change began; a change with which this church, as we have seen, had much to do. It is interesting to read Watson's description of the place in those days, with its "houses of dark, moss-grown stone, and of sombre and prison-like aspect, with little old-fashioned windows, and monstrous corner chimneys formed of stone;" and of its being such a "very long town," with houses in little groups, with intervals between, for several miles along the road; this road itself being in very bad condition generally, so that most of the travel was on horseback. And yet, within 16 years after the date of which he speaks, it was connected with Philadelphia (in 1831) by railway, though not until 1854 did it become, as now, the 22d Ward of that city.

In these various ways, so great a change of population has been effected, that church life is of course, very different from what it was. Comparatively few of the old German families are now to be found in this congregation; and it is no longer the only Presbyterian Church in the place.

Partly from its membership, there was formed in 1852 the Chestnut Hill Church, and in 1857 the Second Church of Germantown. In 1856, the old German Reformed

Congregation had itself become Presbyterian also, connecting itself, however, with the New School body; the other three churches here being Old School. It has been amidst tendencies like these, that the three most recent pastorates have carried on their work. Of these, the first was that of Rev. Henry J. Van Dyke. He was born near Germantown, on the corner of Washington Lane and the Old York Road; studied theology at Princeton, and also under Rev. Albert Barnes and Dr. Brainerd; was ordained and installed pastor of the Second Church, Bridgeton, N. J., in June, 1845, remaining there for the next seven years.

In July, 1852, he was called to this church, and in October following, was installed; the services being in charge of Rev. Dr. William Neill, Rev. Jacob Belville, and Rev. Dr. Robert Steel.

Mr. Van Dyke had not been quite a year in this position, when in May, 1853, he felt constrained to accept the urgent call which had been given him by the First Presbyterian Church in Brooklyn, New York. Since then, he has become widely known and honored as Moderator of the General Assembly, and in other ways. The church in Germantown dismissed him very reluctantly. Some fourteen members were added during his brief stay.

For the next sixteen years, from September, 1853, to July, 1869, the Rev. James H. Mason Knox, D. D., had the pastoral charge. He was born in New York city, educated at Columbia College, and the Theological Seminary at New Brunswick, and licensed by the Classis of New York. His first pastoral charge was at German Valley, N. J., when he was ordained and installed by the Presbytery of Newton: and he afterward removed to the Reformed Dutch Church at Easton, Penna., where a fine building was erected, and paid for during his stay.

He was installed in this church, November 9th, 1853,

his father, Rev. Dr. John Knox, of the Collegiate Reformed Church in New York city, preached the sermon, and Rev. Roger Owen, of Chestnut Hill, giving the charges. This was the longest of all the pastorates, and that which witnessed most of the changes to which we have already referred. Immediately after the coming of Dr. Knox in 1854, extensive alterations were made in the church building, so that for the Sunday School and for evening lectures, there was provision made, in rooms separate from the main audience-room. This was effected by making the edifice consist of two stories, instead of one, as heretofore. On the lower floor, besides the pastor's study, etc., was the Sunday School or Lecture Room, in which there still remained the old-fashioned square pews which had been occupied for so many years in the church services. Their ample space was perhaps more suggestive than the narrower modern slips, of the fact that a church is meant to have as .its members, not individuals merely, but families. The scriptural teaching on that point, however, was not at any time more positive or effective, than during the pastorate in which this change was made.

The body of Sabbath worshippers was thus brought to the upper story, where they were provided with a room of ample height, and were brought at last within easy distance of the pulpit, which had in former years towered far above them in the air. The church building was renewing its youth, and became much more convenient and useful than before.

The improvement in its edifice may be taken as an indication of a corresponding access of new life throughout the church itself. One token of this is found in the very fact that these alterations were undertaken at no less a cost than $7000, which was no small sum for a congregation such as this had been. In fact, it is one of the especial features of this pastorate, frequently recognized as such, that the spirit of liberality in giving to christian enterprises, was so successfully fostered. Instead of being, as at its best estate hitherto, barely self-supporting, or even dependent on the Home Mission Board for assistance, the church became henceforth a generous giver to gospel work outside of its own bounds. This was not merely from the new families who were attracted into its membership, but from the patient and faithful development of this grace in the congregation at large. Contributions increased in far greater proportion than did the wealth of the people, and since the giving was made to depend not on impulse, but on christian and scriptural principle, its results in the people have not been temporary, but life-long; by no means ceasing to bear fruit, even after the removal to another field, of the hand which had given this training. There was raised for religious purposes during the pastorate of Dr. Knox somewhat more than $107,000, of which amount $63,229 were sent to the various missionary and benevolent boards of the church at large. Since this came from growth in grace, and not solely from growth in riches, it is of course good evidence of other spiritual progress, which may not be so easily described in words. Dr. Knox received two hundred and seventy-five persons into membership, and performed one hundred and sixty-eight baptisms.

He resigned his position in July, 1869, and has been for several years in charge of the church in Bristol, Penna., within the same Presbytery as Germantown. His continued interest in this church, and our affectionate remembrance of him, are evidenced continually by the manner in which his presence is invited and welcomed on any occasion of special importance in the life of his old people.

In October, 1869, Rev. J. Frederic Dripps was invited to supply the pulpit, and shortly afterward arrangements were commenced for having him called to the pastoral charge; but at his own request this was postponed for a month, to enable more intelligent action on both sides. At the expiration of this time he was given the call unanimously, on January 3d, 1870.

He was born in Philadelphia, and graduated at the University of the City of New York, and at the Princeton Theological Seminary. In the interval which elapsed after graduation, and before coming to Germantown, he had preached for six months, during the pastor's absence, in the First Presbyterian Church of Indianapolis, and afterward for eight months in the American Presbyterian Church of Montreal, Canada. He was ordained and installed in Germantown, March 7, 1870, Rev. Mr. Beggs presiding as Moderator of the Presbytery; Rev. Dr. John Hall of New York preaching the sermon, Rev. Dr. Withrow (then of Philadelphia) giving the charge to the pastor, and Rev. Dr. Murphy of Frankford, giving that to the people.

One of the earliest movements in the church, under this pastorate, was that which looked toward the erection of a new house of worship. It is pleasant to remember that this step, like so many of those which we have already recorded, came from motives which were not those of worldly ambition, but of sincere desire for more effective work and worship. It is, at times, the case that even when some christian enterprise does end in good, yet its beginning is made under somewhat questionable circumstances; so that a church may be born of dissension, or an edifice erected from the mere spirit of display. It is, therefore, cause for sincere thankfulness to God that we can ascribe to His own grace and guidance this building; even as we can trace to Him the origin of the former building, of the congregation itself, and of the very community in which it is situated.

In April, 1870, the spiritual influence of the communion season continued to show itself in a permanently increased attendance at the usual weekly prayer-meetings, and that to an extent sufficient to produce the necessity for increased accommodations in the lecture-room. A collection was made for this purpose on the 1st of May. On the 17th of May, the Trustees met to arrange for executing the work, but found themselves planning so many other improvements, that they were led to think seriously of erecting an entirely new edifice. This project had encountered so many obstacles whenever attempted previously, that the expectation of success was not at all sanguine. Still, as it seemed to be a plain duty to make the effort, it was undertaken.

One great difficulty had always been that of finding the proper site. The lot occupied by the old building was too irregular in shape to be desirable, and its value for business purposes made its sale expedient. It was not easy, however, to find a new site, satisfactory in other respects, which would be convenient for this widely-scattered congregation, without interfering with any other church. At this precise juncture, a property was offered for the purpose in a manner which we certainly have warrant for considering providential. The property itself had not been for sale before this time, forming, as it did, a large part of the garden attached to a private residence; and even had it been offered to us at any earlier date, there were obstacles on the other side, preventing its acceptance by this church. Every obstacle seemed now to be removed, however, as quickly as presented, and as the site was entirely convenient for the congregation, was on an avenue as desirable as any in Germantown, and was so satisfactory in other respects, the offer was accepted. The congregation formally authorized the sale of the old property and purchase of the new one, July 11. The fall was spent in procuring suitable plans for the building. The time of year when we were enabled to make this decision, was so ordered as exactly to suit both our need of time for full preparation, and our desire to make a start with the very beginning of the building season. The general plans furnished by Mr. James H. Windrim, the architect, being selected, the matter was formally laid before the congregation by the pastor on Sabbath, December 11, and within the week the sum of $20,000 was subscribed. This amount, in addition to the value of the old property, gave so solid a foundation pecuniarily, that Building and Finance Committees were appointed at once, and went vigorously to work.

On the Building Committee were Messrs. T. Charlton Henry, William Adamson, Thomas MacKellar, Enoch Taylor, Woodruff Jones and Thomas H. Garrett; Messrs. Henry, Adamson and MacKellar being given personal supervision of the work.

The Finance Committee consisted of Messrs. James Garrett, James Kinnier, Dr. G. H. Burgin, Jonathan Graham, Charles W. Henry and W. B. MacKellar.

February 16th, the contract was let to Messrs. James Kinnier and Sons, and early in March ground was broken. The nature of the soil threatened to prevent the securing of a good foundation; but, by the marked personal energy of the contractors, every difficulty was overcome, and a solid rock foundation was at last secured for the whole building. From that time, everything went on prosperously, even in little things. The stone, which was from a newly-opened quarry, turned out to be excellent; all the other material proved satisfactory, and the different classes of workmen made such close connection one with another that no time was lost through delays. No injury to life or limb was permitted; the workmen proved to be honest and obliging, and the contractors, by their faithful and disinterested exertions, carried as they were, beyond all that could have been required of them, showed plainly that their chief aim was to present the church of which they had so long been members, with an edifice which would be found thoroughly substantial and satisfying.

Not only in the contractors, and the Building Committee, and the larger subscribers, but throughout the whole mass of the congregation, a spirit of zeal and devotion was manifest throughout the work. All contributions were voluntary, no extraneous means were needed ; the sending out blank subscription cards secured abundant returns. The liberality of these gifts on the part of all classes was the more noticeable, because of the fact that no other part of church work was suffered to flag on account of this. It was, indeed, a period of unusual energy in all kinds of christian work.

The pleasure experienced from the unity and good feeling of the congregation itself, was almost equalled by that which came from the kindly interest and sympathy of the other churches and of the community in general.

An additional favor was shown in enabling us to dispose of the old building in a way so unusually satisfactory ; it was sold to the Young Men's Christian Association of Germantown, under circumstances exceedingly pleasant and gratifying to both parties. In short, the Lord gave help and guidance in every direction, far beyond what was anticipated. On the morning of Sabbath, May 12, 1872, the substance of the foregoing sketch was given to the congregation, in preparation for the farewell service in the old building, which was held on the same evening. The new edifice was used during the next week for a prayer meeting on Wednesday and social meeting on Friday, both held in the "Children's Church," as it was called, and very largely attended. On Sabbath morning, May 19, the first service was held in the church proper, its object being to recognize this building as a gift from God to us; in the evening we solemnly gave it again to Him at the dedication service.

On this occasion there were in the pulpit and participating in the exercises, Rev. J. H. M. Knox, D. D., R. D. Harper, D. D., E. P. Cowan and A. McCullagh, with the pastor of the church, while the congregations of the Market Square, and the Second Presbyterian Churches, and of Trinity Lutheran Church, combined with our own to produce an audience which filled not only the pews, but the aisles and every passage and entrance-hall. The dedicatory prayer was offered by the pastor, and the sermon preached by Rev. Robert D. Harper, D. D., from Haggai ii. 9; Rev. Dr. Knox closing with the benediction from Numbers vii. 24–26. The hymns and anthems were rendered by a large choir under the direction of Mr. Woodruff Jones.

The following is a brief description of the new edifice:

It is situated on the north side of Chelten Avenue, about two hundred feet west of Germantown Avenue, and consists of a church proper with transverse building in the rear for lecture room, etc. The entire length is one hundred and thirty-seven feet, and the extreme width eighty-eight feet; the apex of the roof rising sixty-six feet from the ground, and the spire one hundred and fifty feet. The masonry is of gneiss rock, with selected facings. Two vestibules, at opposite corners of the front, afford entrance to the church proper, which is eighty feet long, fifty-nine feet wide, and forty-four in height to the apex of the ceiling. The organ and choir occupy a raised platform in the alcove between the two front vestibules, the pulpit alcove being at the opposite end of the room. Abundant light is secured during the day, by the large double windows on each side and the rose-window in front, forty feet in circumference; and at night by two large reflectors just below the apex of the ceiling, containing thirty-six burners in each. The whole interior finish is conformed in detail to the style of the building, which is Gothic, of the early decorated type.

The woodwork, including pulpit and organ case, doors and wainscoting, pews and furniture, is of black walnut, finished in oil with smooth glass.

The rear building contains on the ground floor, a lecture room and infant-school room; on the second floor, the main Sunday School room, which is a large and lofty hall, affording a very beautiful "church for the children." Opening from this are the pastor's study and the ladies' parlor, over which is a gallery with alcoves for the Bible classes. The whole effect of this floor is unusually pleasing. Every room and passage in the whole edifice was painted in fresco by Kehrweider Brothers, in the most satisfactory manner.

Especial care has been given to the ventilation: among the means which are used being ducts which have perforated openings through the floor, and communicate with a large ventilating shaft, perforated openings in the ceilings, which can be regulated or closed at will, the usual flues in the walls, etc. The architect was James H. Windrim, Esq., of Philadelphia. A new organ, valued at $4,300, was constructed by the Messrs. Standbridge, of Philadelphia, under the special supervision of Mr. Woodruff Jones, in readiness for the dedication services. In exterior appearance and in quality of tone, it is all that could be desired.

The total cost of the building and furniture was $70,296.00. Of this amount, $21,564.00, came from the sale of the old building and organ, leaving $48,732.00 as the amount paid in cash by the congregation. The entire valuation of the property is $79,796.00, which includes $9,500 for the ground; this however, was taken upon a mortgage, having several years before maturity.

So far as the edifice itself is concerned, including furniture, etc., the arrangements were so made, that payments were distributed over two or three successive years; and in due time every cent was paid in full. This was almost wholly accomplished by those who had been with us when the work began, for during the execution of such an enterprise, a church can hardly expect to receive any large accessions to its membership from outside. Those who did join us at that time, however, took up at once their full share with the rest. Subscriptions were made at the beginning of each year during the work, being sent to the Trustees upon cards, furnished for that purpose. Payments were made in advance, either weekly, monthly or quarterly, as preferred by the subscriber. And they came in from all classes, rich and poor, adults and children.

More than one family from whom five dollars would have been counted a fair gift, sent in this way over fifty dollars in weekly instalments. The poorest member who could give but five or ten cents a week, felt the new church to be his own, as really as the giver of thousands did; and with good reason, for each gave his own proper share.

No fairs were held, and no appeals made, except the mere statement from time to time, usually but once a year, of the amount needed; and so far as the pastor was concerned, these annual statements included all the service which was asked of him, in connection with the raising of money.

In addition to the money which was thus cheerfully given, even during the time of commercial disaster, which came on before the payments were finished, many valuable articles were presented by different members, in token of special interest and affection. Altogether, the erection of this building was not only a fruit of grace, but very decidedly a means of grace in every way. There are only grateful and pleasant associations connected with it.

It may be well to mention in this connection, the fact that before entering the new edifice, a change of plan for meeting the current annual expenses was adopted.

On the 3d of April, 1872, after considering the subject at two meetings, in successive weeks, the congregation voted to leave it to each member to decide for himself how much he would pay toward church expenses, instead of having it decided for him by the committee on pew rents. This was not done with any idea of calling this a "free church," nor was any particular name given to the plan, but it was felt that the change from one church building to another, gave a suitable opportunity for arranging this matter in a way which commended itself as more desirable than the former method.

Accordingly, it was agreed that each person or family attending the church should be assigned a permanent seat or pew, on which their name should be kept so long as they continued regularly to occupy it. The ownership and control of each pew remains, however, with the church itself, and not with the occupant; no person has any claim upon a seat beyond the time during which he regularly uses it. No price has ever been charged for a seat, and no rent was ever assessed. Each regular attendant is of course expected to bear his own share of the common expense, bnt it has been honestly left to the person himself to decide what that share is. At the beginning of each year a printed estimate of the amount which will be required for the next twelve months, is distributed among the congregation, and then blank subscription cards are sent to each person. These are filled out by the persons themselves, who thereby undertake, so far as God shall enable them, to pay a certain amount each week, or month, or quarter, during the year, but the contents of these subscription cards are not made public. The money is paid at the beginning of each week, or month, &c., by inclosing the proper amount in one of the envelopes sent for the purpose, (each of them having upon it certain figures, which indicate to the Treasurer whose it is), and dropping the envelope into the box near the entrance door of the church. It is not known that any person has ever taken unfair advantage of this plan, but on the contrary, far larger amounts were brought in, when each member felt that his share was to be fixed according to the impulse of his own heart and conscience.

In the first year, instead of $2000, which had been the largest sum ever paid for pew-rents, some $4600 were subscribed and paid; next year the amount was $5600, and it has continued to be from $5500 to $6000 since then. Great satisfaction is felt with this plan. It prevents any possibility of having pews in the house of God sold like real estate in the public market, to buyers who may have none but a pecuniary interest in them. It retains full control over every seat in the hands of the church itself. It has relieved persons who could not continue to pay as largely as in former years, from any need to explain or apologize, or ask indulgence, since they are always at liberty to adjust their subscription to their means as a matter of right. Should the total amount subscribed prove inadequate, a statement to that effect would be made to the whole congregation, and an increase of so much per

cent. on each subscription would be requested. The
response to this appeal also would be voluntary, but it has
proved none the less reliable on that account.

Another subject, closely connected with this, which also
received careful ₁attention for some years, was that of
systematic beneficence; *i. e.*, the collecting of money, not
for the operations of the congregation itself, but for outside
objects of a missionary or charitable nature. The year in
which this pastorate began was the same as that which
witnessed the Re-union between Old School and New
School; and that event was followed by much effort to
increase and systematize benevolent contributions. So far
as this particular church is concerned, no change was
made in the method formerly used.

One Sabbath in the year is designated for a collection in
behalf of each of those regular objects of benevolence,
which are under the charge of the Boards of the Presbyterian
Church. Notice is always given to the congregation on
the preceding Sabbath, and a careful explanation of the
object for which money is asked, is given at the time by the
pastor. The contributions are received in plates handed
around as usual, and before being finally sent off, the
collection is retained in the Treasurer's hands for a week,
in order that any persons who were not present at the time
may send in their gifts to him. This latter opportunity is
constantly used, and the plate collection is considerably
increased by the sums voluntarily sent in by those who
were absent or unprepared when it was taken.

It has been found by experience, that this plan com-
mends itself by its results, quite as well as some far more
elaborate methods which were proposed to us; and it
should be understood that our disinclination to change is
the result, not at all of neglecting to examine these other
plans, but of finding them not so satisfactory to us as the

old way. For example, one system frequently suggested, was that of asking each member to subscribe in advance, whatever sum he could, for external benevolent purposes in general, during the year; the total amount so raised, being then divided by the Session among the various Boards, in proportion to their respective claims. This was called by its advocates "The Systematic Plan," but the advantages which it claimed have been secured quite as well by the old system. The "Plate Collection" is as really a system, with regular results, as this other scheme. It does not, in our experience, leave the amount for each Board to be reduced indefinitely by such casualties as the occurrence of stormy weather on the collection Sabbath, for, as stated above, all the larger givers, and many of the others, are in the habit of sending in their gifts afterward, if prevented at the time. It was claimed for the new scheme, that it made christian giving to be matter of principle, and not dependent on the impulse of special appeals; but it is difficult to see why principle may not be aided, as well as impulse, by an explanation from the pulpit, of each particular object, at the time when it is presented for contributions. And the new plan was felt by us to be "systematic" in a very objectionable way, when it interfered with the freedom of individual christians to decide the proportion in which they would devote their voluntary offerings to one and another form of the Lord's work. Every person and every church, has an individuality of its own, with which this general scheme, with its fixed percentages, was felt to be in conflict. The same end, so far as it is desirable, has been gained by simply explaining to the people the claims of each Board in its turn, and leaving to them the proportioning of their gifts.

The sum total of contributions made by this church for religious and benevolent purposes, within the last ten years, exceeds $175,000: more than that sum having already been contributed at the beginning of December, 1879. Of this amount, over $73,000 were given to objects outside of the church itself, such as Home and Foreign Missions, etc. It is cause of gratitude to God, that He has so maintained the grace of liberality within this people, that during a decade in which they could not help feeling the commercial depression of the times, their gifts for religion were increased and not diminished. This has been effected without resorting to fairs, and similar questionable expedients: against which there has always been a strong feeling in the church. The giving has been from principle, and with every indication of that cheerfulness which God has pronounced well-pleasing to Him.

The regular annual collections for those departments of christian work, which are carried on by the Boards of our Church, are arranged in the following order, viz.:

In January, ... Foreign Missions.
February, ... Education.
March, ... Sustentation.
May, ... Publication.
September, ... Church Erection.
October, ... Ministerial Relief.
November, ... · Home Missions.
December, ... Freedmen.

There is another department of church life which claims attention on the record, namely, that of personal and active effort. One of our earliest movements in this direction, during the last decade, was the organization of the Ladies' Pastoral Aid Society. This took place on the 20th of April, 1870.

There was already in existence a Domestic Mission

Society, which had been for eighteen years sending boxes to Home missionaries; and a Bible-readers' Society, with Mother's Meetings under its care: besides which, Dorcas Meetings were held, and collections were made by visitors for the Women's Union Foreign Mission Society. It was important that this Foreign Mission work should be regularly organized and extended, that systematic visiting should be undertaken, and the way opened for still other forms of work. Yet it was evidently undesirable to indefinitely multiply separate organizations. The endeavor was therefore made to form a Union of these societies, of such a kind that each could be unfettered in doing its own work, and yet have opportunity for meeting all the others, at regular intervals, for mutual council and aid. This Union or Association could have supervision over all the various societies of which it was formed, by means of a central Executive Committee, while it would in reality be not so much another new society, but rather a combination of those which already existed.

In all but name, this is the precise thing which was done. The new organization was called the Pastoral Aid Society, and each of the societies which combined to form it, had its title changed to that of "Standing Committee." But the "Bible-reader's Committee" continued to have every power which it had possessed while it was called the "Bible-reader's Society;" it did the same work, had the same officers, and was, within itself, entirely the same as before. The only new feature was in its external relations; it had agreed to unite with the other committees, and to give general supervision of its affairs to this Union. The supervision, however, was hardly more than nominal, for its sole object was to advise and help, if necessary, but not to constrain. As a matter of fact, not only this, but every other committee, has conducted its own

affairs, at meetings of its own, as freely as though no
Pastoral Aid Society existed. The work of each has been
the more energetic, and not the less so, because of its
connection with all the rest. . Experience has shown the
plan to be easily worked and efficient. Many new forms
of work have been carried into successful operation, which
would not have been undertaken but for the help afforded
by this Society, and the older, more familiar work, has
been not only sustained but enlarged.

There has been the utmost degree of freedom for individual impulse, and for gratifying personal inclination
toward particular kinds of activity, consistent with the
benefits of orderly combination and harmony. Whatever
sort of christian effort may elicit the interest of any woman
in the church, she can find in this Society a ready means
of enlisting others to help her, and of forming thus a
committee for that particular object. This committee can
give information of its condition and needs at every
Pastoral Aid Meeting, and thus secure sympathy and aid,
while at the same time it is given enough of supervision to
keep it from interfering with other and older committees.
Obviously, no harm is to be apprehended from multiplying
indefinitely the number of such organizations, for they
pre-suppose in every case a group of christian women,
interested spontaneously in some particular enterprise,
which they undertake to carry out in such a way as to
refrain from any possible clashing with the other enterprises
which are already in operation.

It should also be noticed that the whole work represented
by this society is under the immediate supervision of the
Church Session, as its Constitution provides ; and that
nothing of importance has ever been undertaken in connection with it until after full consultation with the pastor.
The name of the Society was indeed chosen by the Ladies

present at the organization, expressly to indicate their intentions in this matter.

The system itself was so arranged that it might, if possible, continue in operation without needing any essential change: adapting itself to any future emergency which might arise. It is inherently flexible enough to admit of every single committee being discontinued, one after another, if any necessity of that kind may be imagined, and wholly new forms of work taken up; while meantime the Society itself still binds together whatever committees do exist. A copy of the "Constitution and By-Laws," as given in the Annual Report for 1879, will be found in the Appendix to this volume; it will be seen that simplicity and brevity have been sought in preparing them.

A sketch of the various Standing Committees and their work will now be given. It may be well to prefix the remark, that the present number of Committees has been attained only by degrees, in the course of several years; the Society began with comparatively few of them, and would have been well worth organizing even for its benefit to these, and apart from any idea of forming new ones.

THE STANDING COMMITTEE ON DOMESTIC MISSIONS

has continued the work of the Domestic Missionary Society, which was founded in 1852, for the purpose of sending relief to needy missionaries under the care of the Presbyterian Board. The aggregate value of the boxes sent by it up to 1870, was about $10,000. In order to promote the efficiency of church work, it connected itself with the Pastoral Aid Society, on May 4th, 1870: retaining the same President, Secretary and Treasurer, and the same membership as before. In the last ten years, boxes valued at $6,000, have been prepared and sent out. The venerable servants of God who began this work, have shown unfailing interest and devotion for these twenty-seven years, gathering up $16,000 worth of supylies, carefully chosen and adapted to the special needs of each case. Their correspondence with the Home Missionaries receiving these boxes, has sometimes continued for years afterward; and a relation of permanent friendliness and interest on both sides, has frequently resulted.

A glance over any of the letters, taken at random from the large collection which remains in possession of the Committee, will satisfy any one of the great good which has been done by this work. In fact, this is so very obvious, that there is little room for giving any explanations concerning a form of Christian effort to be found among so many of our churches.

The Committee is in the habit of securing the names of several Missionaries from the Board, or from other sources, and selecting those which appear most desirable for correspondence and help. Request is then made, through a notice from the pulpit, for suitable gifts in material or in money; whatever sewing may be needful, being done by the individual givers at their own convenience. When the Committee next meets, it is to receive and pack these articles, always with special united prayer to God, for His lessing upon givers and receivers alike. On these occasions, which are always attended with much that is interesting, the presence of any fellow-members of the church is very welcome.

THE STANDING COMMITTEE ON FOREIGN MISSIONS

began operations with the first business meeting of the Pastoral Aid Society, May 4th, 1870. During the year preceding this, some of the ladies had begun to make collections for the Woman's Union Mission Society; which was of course done with the understanding that this should not interfere with the usual contribution to Foreign Missions by the congregation at large. But it was felt that the time had come for enlarging the Woman's Work, if possible; and at the meeting above mentioned, this committee was appointed, with the intention of having it take into consideration the whole subject. Its more immediate object was, to represent this church at a convention held the same month in Philadelphia, preliminary to the organization of the Woman's Foreign Mission Society of the Presbyterian Church. That organization did not take place for several months, however; and meantime the ladies in this church had become still more deeply interested than before, in the Woman's Union Foreign Mission Society, and had agreed to contribute to it for the next five years, through the Germantown Auxiliary, which had been formed January 19, 1869. This pledge was fulfilled by contributions for the support of Miss Hook in India. No further pledge was given, at the expiration of that time; but gifts for this society have been received and sent to it yearly, and it is hoped that this will continue to be the case. It is to the Union Society that we as a church owe the first quickening of interest in this great branch of Woman's work; it was through its success, achieved under all the difficulties which attend pioneer work, that the other and more strictly denominational societies were encouraged to organize; and the knowledge of its effectiveness on the Foreign field, combines with our sense of gratitude for its past services, and reverence for the memory of its sainted founder, Mrs. Doremus, to secure from us the continuance of hearty interest and good will. Contributions are received for this object, either through the usual collectors or through the Treasurer of the Committee. The amount of such contributions, up to the first of April, 1879, was $1,019.95.

The greater part of our work, however, has been carried on through the Woman's Foreign Mission Society of the Presbyterian Church. As already stated, this committee took part in the movements connected with the formation of that society; but did not complete the relation thus begun until 1872. In November of that year, a meeting was held in the Lecture-room, to receive statements in regard to the work carried on by the women of the Presbyterian Church in heathen lands. So much interest was felt in the addresses made on behalf of that society, and especially in the facts with regard to Japan, that a second meeting was at once held, and after conference with the other ladies in the church, this Committee undertook the duties of an Auxiliary to the Presbyterian Society, and the responsibility of furnishing the entire support for a missionary in Japan. It was proposed that Miss Gamble, who had spent some years with her brother in China, where he was connected with the mission work of our Board, should become our representative at Tokio. She consented so to do, and preparations for her outfit were at once begun.

Delays occurred, however, which prevented her leaving this country for nearly a year. Meantime the ladies secured from her as many visits as possible, in order to make the new relation more full of personal acquaintance and sympathy: she became, at her own suggestion, a member of this church, and by the time of her departure had been made to feel very much at home in it. A farewell meeting was held on Wednesday evening, October 15, 1873, and the next day Miss Gamble left for Japan, where she arrived safely on the 30th of November. From this time the contributions were materially increased. In 1870, the amount of our contribution for the Union Society was $75; in 1871, it was $120; and in 1872, it was $202. In 1873, besides sending $175 to that cause, $600 were given for Miss Gamble's outfit, and $125 towards securing for the school in Tokio, (to which place she went) a cabinet organ. In the course of the following year, her work was interrupted, in part by ill health, and a few months later her connection with us was terminated by her departure to China, where her relations have since that time been with another denomination.

Another lady, the wife of Rev. W. M. K. Imbrie, was suggested in her place, but she felt herself obliged to decline, on the ground that for the time she was not able to undertake anything beyond her home duties. Even before her letter reached us, the Board of Missions had taken action which would in any case have interfered with this arrangement, by assigning the field of Tokio, where Mrs. Imbrie resides, to the New York Society, and that of Yokohama to our Philadelphia Society. This change involved a re-adjustment of our plans, which occupied some time. In November, 1876, however, arrangements were completed by which Mrs. John Ballagh became our missionary after January 1st of the following year. Since that time, a fresh impulse has been given to the work in all directions, by the helpful and quickening influence which comes from intercourse with this faithful and devoted servant of God.

It is well to notice, that during the four years which immediately followed our entrance upon this work, we were carrying it on as matter of principle, without dependence upon the stimulus of regular correspondence with a missionary; for until we knew Mrs. Ballagh, there was but a very brief time during which any letter at all came to us from the foreign field.

The lack of this stimulus was indeed felt; and especially by those contributors to whom the Woman's Foreign

Work was entirely a new one. But there was always enough of interest in the work for its own sake, and apart from all craving for the sight of immediate results, to secure its continuance without any deficiency.

The contributions which have been made through this committee, as an auxiliary of the Presbyterian Society, amounted, on the 1st of April, 1879, to $3980.95 : adding to this the $1019.95 given to the Union Society, a total is produced of $5000 secured for Foreign Mission Work through this organization up to that time. This includes the cost of a cabinet organ sent for Mrs. Ballagh's school in 1879.

At the beginning, some fears were expressed that these gifts would interfere with the annual contribution from the congregation at large to the Mission Board, but the result has been of a very different kind ; a wider and deeper interest in the whole work of missions has been secured, so that, beside other good results, the annual collection (which does not include any of the sums above referred to) has risen from $462 in 1870, to more than $1000 in 1879 : ($890 being sent to the Board, and the remainder to the Mexican Mission.)

At this point, some words as to the organization of the Committee will be in place. Its membership is divided into two classes, Contributing and Active. The contributing members include all the ladies who give regularly to the support of the work and are members of the church. The Active members are those who are entrusted with the the management of the work itself. The members of this latter class were chosen at first by the pastor, in conference with the Pastoral Aid officers ; the object being to secure persons specially interested in missions, and willing to give the required time and trouble. Their numbers are maintained since then, by having the Committee itself nominate and elect new members from time to time, subject to revision by the contributors. A report of all such proceedings is provided for : it is to be made to the contributing members each year, at the annual meeting of the Pastoral Aid Society, where they are expected to be present. It is also understood that during the year, in case the Committee is contemplating any unusual action, of such importance as to make proper a conference with the contributors, report of the same can be made at any Pastoral Aid meeting, and a vote taken thereon. Practically, therefore, so far as the business meetings are concerned, the Committee consists of these "Active members." They elect annually a President, Secretary, and Treasurer.

These officers represent the Committee in its intercourse with various external bodies, such as the Woman's Union Society, the Presbyterian Society, and that branch of the same which is composed of the churches in this particular Presbytery. The meetings for transaction of business are held monthly, during most of the year. Arrangements are made for having collectors, who call upon the regular contributors at stated intervals, and deliver the sums which are given them, together with the names of the persons contributing, to the Treasurer.

That officer reports at each regular meeting, so that the committee may be fully acquainted with the condition of the Treasury, and may from time to time secure new subscribers to the list. The Secretary preserves a copy of this roll of contributors and amounts, with the names of collectors, etc. Another part of her duties, in addition to the keeping of minutes, etc., is the copying of letters from our missionary into a suitable book, that they may be kept for reference. Many such letters have been received by different members which contain matter of permanent interest, and meant for the information of all, but which, after being once handed around for perusal, are practically inaccessible, unless secured on record in this way. It is understood, of course, that any thing which is intended by Mrs. Ballagh solely for the particular person to whom a letter is addressed, shall be omitted from the copy. All this correspondence is in addition to that which is carried on officially by the Secretary; and in this fact is seen one of the many tokens which evidence Mrs. Ballagh's overflowing zeal for the work, and her readiness to stimulate the zeal of others.

One result of the increased interest which has been awakened by her influence, is the formation of several additional Mission Bands. These are under the general supervision of this Committee, which receives their reports and gives them all possible aid and encouragement.

The first in order of formation, is that called "Willing Workers for Jesus," organized in 1876, by some of the younger girls. They sent a box of materials for fancy work to Mrs. Hepburn's school, where such gifts were very serviceable for their effect in interesting the scholars. In the fall of 1877, they sent a supply of hymn books for Mrs. Ballagh's school, and in the winter a box of sewing materials valued at $82.

The Band was able to interest the Infant School of the church, and also the Pulaskiville Sunday School, in preparing this box, so that many a little offering was brought with eager interest by children whose earthly possessions were meagre enough. The Band has given more than $140 in cash for the support of children at school in Japan, and still another box, more valuable than any preceding one, was sent in October, 1879.

It holds monthly meetings, at which various items of missionary news are read by different members, and also letters from some of the scholars abroad with whom a correspondence is maintained. In December, 1878, it held a very interesting meeting for young people, at which a large audience gathered to hear Mr. Ono, a Japanese gentleman, and to examine the many curiosities which have been sent from time to time by Mrs. Ballagh and other friends.

Four other Bands have been formed, by as many different classes in our Sunday Schools; namely, those taught by Mrs. S. M. Justice, at Somerville, and by Mrs. M. D. Westcott in the Home School, the Home Infant School, and one at Pulaskiville. The "S. M. Justice" Band has shown much of self-denying devotion to the cause; the "Crusaders," formed by boys under Mrs. Westcott's care, entered at once into correspondence with some Japanese boys in Mr. Ballagh's school, whose letters have proved uncommonly interesting; and in various other ways good results have been secured through these and the other Bands.

The largest of these Bands, however, is that called the "Watchers," which was organized January 20th, 1870, for young ladies over sixteen years of age. There are now forty-five names on the roll, and very unusual interest has been shown in its operations by the members and their friends. Every month a meeting is held, at which there is great variety and animation in the exercises. Carefully written articles are brought in and read by those to whom they had been assigned; the subject being often some particular aspect of the mission field for the month, such as the history of the nation, its geographical and commercial relations, the progress of Christianity, the nature, history or present condition of its heathen religion, etc. At other times more general subjects have been taken. Both in this and in every other feature of the Band work, most encouraging results have been secured by the watchful interest of the Leader, who first makes herself familiar with it all, and then is able to give any needful guidance to the members, without in any way doing their work for them.   The effort is to enlist as many different persons as possible, and make use of whatever peculiar talent each may have.   Much interest was shown during the first year in preparing large maps of the various mission-fields, each of them drawn on muslin with neatness and accuracy. These were soon brought into use in the church mission meetings and elsewhere, besides rendering great assistance to the Band.

Some of the members are especially charged with caring for the music at these meetings, including not only the usual hymns, but anything else that may be appropriate and feasible.   Others bring in various brief items illustrating heathen life or mission work, taken from any book or paper with which they have met since the last meeting. Still others help to prepare suitable Bible-readings.   In all these ways, and by recitations, etc., something is found for every willing hand to do.   Those who do not care to undertake a composition of their own, will act as copyists for others.   A "Mission Band Post-office" is also in successful operation, so that any who would not otherwise make remarks or suggestions, or even inquiries, may write anything of the kind and have it read by the Leader, who, of course, does not give the writer's name.

It will be seen, therefore, that one great object of the Band is to train all its members into the habit of reading for themselves the great facts connected with Foreign Missions.   It is believed that in any church there may be many persons who will drop money into a collection plate, where there are comparatively few who give, in addition to this, an intelligent sympathy and earnest prayerfulness. Such training as this which is here attempted, will not only tend to secure money, but to produce new missionaries, and to fill those who remain at home with the true mission spirit.

The Band is not meant, however, to neglect those contributions to the mission treasury which are always so welcome. Arrangements are made for enabling any who wish so to do, to earn money of their own for this purpose, by copying, or by doing fancy work and sewing for ladies who require it. Orders are sent through the Band officers. This may open the way for very pleasant sewing meetings.

A prayer-meeting is held every month by the Band, to which only those are invited who are willing to take part themselves in its exercises, so that there may be no spirit of criticism, but only that of mutual sympathy and help. These services have been of great benefit.

THE STANDING COMMITTEE ON BIBLE READERS WORK.

This continues the work of the Bible Reader's Association, which was formed in the Spring of 1868, and connected itself with the Pastoral Aid Society on the 4th of May, 1870. The Mother's Meeting was originated by this Committee. Mrs. Baldwin acted as Bible Reader from March to November 1868; Mrs. Sarah McNeill, from January 1869 to April 1873, and from Dec. 1874 to Nov. 1878; Miss Mary A. Williams holding the position during the period when Mrs. McNeill was matron of the Woman's Christian Association, from Nov. 1873 to Dec. 1874. Miss E. A. Hawley held the position from February to December, 1879, and Mrs. C. D. Scott is the present incumbent. There has therefore been very little interruption to this work since it began.

Relief to bodily need was at first included among its objects, but experience has led to the separation of this from the other part of the work. Cases for relief are now reported by the Bible Reader to another Committee, while her own work is kept distinct from alms-giving. Each of the ladies named above, has taken the position in the true mission spirit, accepting only salary enough to supplement other means of support. Four afternoons a week are usually spent in visiting. The methods used are various, of course: they include the reading of the Bible itself, religious conversation, especially concerning the benefits of Christianity in the temptations and trials of daily life, with the reading and distribution of tracts and religious papers, etc. The Bible Reader goes as a Christian woman to do that kind of good, which only woman can with effectiveness do. She visits among the families in the congregation, not merely in cases of sickness and poverty, but wherever as a Christian friend she has access. There are on the outskirts of the congregation, many scores of families who look to this church for religious influence more than to any other, although not in any regular connection even here: the children being usually in attendance upon one of our Sunday-Schools. Among all these she visits, and also among those who are outside of all the churches. In case they most naturally belong to some other church, their attention is turned toward it, and every precaution is taken against even the appearance of proselytism.

The work among these families who are beyond all church influences, was at first the only object in view: but in the course of time, so many of them came into the congregation, while still needing these ministrations of the Bible Reader, that much of her effort is now turned in this direction. In some years a thousand visits would be made, in others, not more than half that number, according to circumstances. But enough is always done to render this one of our most valuable agencies.

THE STANDING COMMITTEE ON MOTHERS' MEETINGS.

The Bible-reader found Mothers closely kept at home, with little social pleasure and less spiritual opportunities.

They were invited to meet once a week, and spend an afternoon or evening together sewing, while one of the committee read from some interesting story, closing with devotional exercises; every opportunity being used for informal conversation on spiritual things, especially on household Christianity.

The sewing itself was also helpful. At first the material worked upon, was sold them at cost, payable in weekly instalments; more lately the work of sewing, was itself accepted as payment, at the rate of twenty-five cents for each two hours' meeting.

A few kinds of groceries are furnished, if preferred, instead of the material sewed upon, also at cost (wholesale).

THE STANDING COMMITTEE ON DORCAS WORK.

This was originally a Sewing Society, meeting at the church every Friday morning, to sew for the poor, especially for the children of the mission schools, and the cases reported by the Bible-reader.

For some years past, the members have only met together for arranging the distribution; all the sewing being done at home. Garments are now bought already made, or material is bought and distributed to be made up, and then given away.

THE STANDING COMMITTEE ON RELIEF OF THE POOR.

This committee was organized by desire of the Pastor and Elders, who felt that this important department of church work would be well cared for by the christian women, who already were doing so efficiently other work of the same kind.

The membership of the committee is always small, and any changes in it are made after special conference with the Pastor. Experience has fully justified the expectations with which it was organized; the work has been performed with discreetness, and at the. same time with warm sympathy and entire faithfulness. The fund is contributed by the congregation every Communion Day, in ample amount.

THE STANDING COMMITTEE ON TRACTS.

A committee, small in numbers, and of approved judgment, has it in charge to select Tracts for the Bible-reader's use, and also for the Visiting Committees, who carry around a fresh tract to all our families at each visit. The cost is paid by imposing a fine of ten cents on each member of the Pastoral Aid Society, who is absent from any of its meetings, and giving the sum thus raised to this committee.

THE STANDING COMMITTEE ON THE PULASKIVILLE SUNDAY SCHOOL.

This mission school, and also that at Somerville, are included among the work of the Pastoral Aid Society, because each of them was founded by ladies belonging to the Society, and the money for defraying current expenses has usually been collected by them.

Of course, the schools are organized as usual, each under a superintendent and officers of its own, annually chosen by the teachers; this election, and all the proceedings in the schools, being always subject to the revision and control of the Church Session. Yet the connection of the schools with the Pastoral Aid Society is still maintained through the committees; they make known in this way any need which can be supplied by the women of the church, and especially make it their business, as above stated, to collect the money for ordinary expenses.

It was in the same way that a great part of the money necessary for erecting the school buildings was collected.

At Pulaskiville there was evidently need of such a work as this. The district known by that name is indeed small in size, measuring less than two squares in each direction, but it is estimated to contain some eight hundred souls. And although the place is within a half mile of several churches, its inhabitants greatly needed to have the gospel brought to their own doors.

The neighborhood was but recently settled, when its necessities were brought home in various ways to two different ladies of this church, Mrs. Jonathan Graham and Miss Mary Mansfield; they conferred together, and on September 26, 1870, canvassed Pulaskiville for scholars. Pledges were given of the attendance of forty-eight children, and two rooms in a private house were offered for use by the proposed school. Mr. Isaac C. Jones, Jr., agreed to act as Superintendent, and other church families in the part of Germantown nearest Pulaskiville became active in the work. The ladies among them were formally organized as a Standing Committee, by the Pastoral Aid Society, on the 5th of October. October 9th, the Sunday-school met for the first time, with forty-eight scholars and eight teachers. The two rooms were only twelve feet square, and as no others were procurable, the need of a new building was felt at once. The appeal for contributions came at the very time when the church was just undertaking the heavy responsibility of erecting a new edifice for its own use, but it was felt that the mission work would be a help and not a hindrance to the church, and the amount asked for was cheerfully given. There was great need of haste, for the rooms used, meantime, were too small to allow the use of a stove, in the cold days of November; and on Saturday, December 9th, the new chapel was dedicated. On the next day it was occupied by the school.

At the Ninth Anniversary, in October, 1879, there were 18 teachers and 160 scholars on the roll. Of this number, there were 36 scholars who had been present every Sabbath during the year; 9 of them having been present for two years, and 11 for three years, without a single interruption. Such evidences of faithfulness, and permanent interest in the school, are steadily increasing from year to year.

The Standing Committee on Parish School.

This work was organized to meet a need which existed for several years in the Pulaskiville district. It was so crowded with children, that for a long time no room was found for them in the public schools of the vicinity, and they were growing up largely destitute of instruction. From 1871 until 1875, therefore, a daily Parish School was held by the ladies of this Committee, in the Sunday-school chapel at Pulaskiville. For most of this time it was taught by Miss Dalzell, a member of one of our sister churches, and one who showed herself uncommonly devoted and efficient.

A sewing-school was also held on Friday afternoons, by five of the ladies who were able to give personal attendance. The roll of daily attendants at first contained the names of 30 children, but the number was afterward more than doubled. The teacher's salary, and other expenses, were provided by distributing the amount among the twenty members of the Committee, each of whom then secured the requisite subscriptions by personal effort. Arrangements were also made to have a sub-committee of two ladies act as visiting-committee for the week, all the members taking this charge in turn. The teaching was given in the true spirit of the christian Home Missionary, and only a small salary was accepted. After some three years Miss Dalzell was obliged to resign the work from ill-health, to the great regret of all connected with it. The place was not an easy one to fill, and several changes were made during the following year. At the end of this time, as new. public schools had been erected, and the most pressing need of this work no longer existed, it was discontinued. While it was carried on, the usefulness of it was most manifest; daily religious instruction was given, and the influence of the Sunday-school was carried into every day in the week.

It may be well to add that a nominal charge of five cents weekly, was made for each scholar, with good effects upon children and parents.

THE STANDING COMMITTEE ON COTTAGE MEETINGS.

In the spring and summer of 1874, a few ladies of the Society found their way open to hold meetings on Thursday afternoons at Pulaskiville, going from house to house in turn. The good accomplished was unmistakable, but the oppressive heat finally stopped the work for that season, and the pressure of other duties prevented their being resumed in the fall. Other meetings, however, with similar aims, have supplied their place in good measure, from time to time. The very brevity of this record illustrates the elasticity of the Society's plan. Even the smallest group of members can have its work recognized and included within the regular operations of the Church, so as to receive the sympathy and support of the whole body, while there is the most entire freedom for individual action.

THE STANDING COMMITTEE ON SOMERVILLE SUNDAY-SCHOOL

This School is connected with the Society in much the same way as that at Pulaskiville. One of the ladies who founded that school, had in 1874, removed to the eastern part of Germantown, and found still further east, at the Township line, and beyond it, a district composed of outlying settlements, several of which were quite distant from any church whatever. A large part of the inhabitants were losing any habits of church-going which they may formerly have had, and the need of mission work was palpable. The field was canvassed for scholars by this lady, Mrs. Jonathan Graham, August 17, 1874, and twenty-seven names were secured. The refusal of a new Hall, which was to be erected in Somerville, had already been secured by Mr. Graham for the Sunday-School, should one be organized. Efforts were then made to secure other helpers in the work, and on Sept. 8th, a conference was held with Mr. Geo. Wiggan as to his undertaking the superintendency. This gentleman was in the immediate neighborhood, and had formerly been for some time a pew-holder in our church. so that although now a member of the Second Church, he was well known among us, and none the less welcome because he represented the fraternal interest of that congregation in our work.

On September 14th, a report of all this was made to our Session, at its first meeting after the summer vacation, with the information that action had been taken thus far, on the assumption of Sessional approval; and application was made to have their enterprise recognized as a work of this church, under the formal charge of its Pastor and Elders. This application would have been made earlier, but for the absence of several members of Session from town

during the summer. As it was, the proposal received, of
course, the ready sanction which it sought; the new opportunity for work was thankfully welcomed, and by formal
vote of Session, was recognized as regularly under its care,
with the promise of all possible help from the congregation
at large. In the course of the following season, there was
a movement looking toward the establishment of a new
Presbyterian Church between Somerville and Germantown,
at the corner of Penn and Chew Streets, in which case it
was desired to have the Somerville Sunday-School removed
to that point. The proposed church was to be under
charge of the Sessional Union, representing the four
churches of Germantown, but so many difficulties were
encountered, that the enterprise was entirely abandoned.
The new Sunday-School has always remained, therefore, as
it began, a mission school of this church. So few of the
congregation resided within reach of the new field, that
some weeks were occupied in finding the requisite number
of teachers. Ou Oct. 25th, 1874, however, it was fully
organized and held its first service with 48 scholars and 9
scholars. During 1875, the school continued to use the
public Hall in which it had started, at the corner of
Stenton Avenue and Mill Street. In the Spring of 1876,
the necessity for a new building led to the purchase of a
lot, and the beginning of the desired chapel. The
ladies of the Pastoral Aid Committee continued to render
efficient service in procuring the requisite funds, and with
gratifying success. On June 11th, 1876, the "Somerville
Chapel of the First Presbyterian Church " was dedicated,
free of debt. Its erection and furnishing cost $3,235.25,
and the sum of $432.64 in addition, was raised for the
Sunday-School and other services held during the year.
The Sunday-Schools of our three sister churches, gave $50
each toward the erection fund, and the residents in the

vicinity of the School, $504. At the last Anniversary held in October, 1879, there were on the roll, 25 teachers and 278 scholars. The growth of the School is only limited by the size of the building.

THE STANDING COMMITTEE ON PRESBYTERIAN HOME FOR WIDOWS.

This is one of those committees, whose object is to serve as a regular means of communication between the ladies of this church, and any of the benevolent institutions in the neighborhood which may have dealings with them.

The committee usually consists of those members of the society who are, in some way, officially connected with the institution.

In this particular case, it has been enabled to communicate much desirable information to the church, and to secure many subscriptions from our people, for this most valuable Home.

THE STANDING COMMITTEE ON WOMAN'S CHRISTIAN ASSOCIATION.

Those managers of the association, who are also members of this church, form a committee, with the purpose above described. One of them served for some years as President of the Association, and its work is one of great interest to us all.

THE STANDING COMMITTEE ON HOSPITALS.

There are ladies in the Society who are officially connected with the Presbyterian Hospital, and also with the Germantown Hospital. They serve as the organ of communication in all matters pertaining to Woman's work in these directions.

THE STANDING COMMITTEE ON SYSTEMATIC VISITING.

This is a branch of work within the congregation itself, which really occasioned the formation of the Pastoral Aid Society. The Pastor was very desirous of aid from the ladies of the congregation, in keeping all of its families constantly reminded of their relation to the church ; and as other departments of usefulness were also to be opened, there was danger of a multiplication of unconnected societies, which might prove troublesome. Provision was made, therefore, not merely for the desired visiting, but also for combining this and the other new enterprises, with the already-established forms of woman's work, in one organization.

This particular committee is arranged as follows. The whole parish is divided into districts of convenient size, of which there were at first nine, and are now fifteen.

Each of these districts is assigned to a sub-committee of two visitors, who are expected ordinarily to call upon every church-family within its bounds, once in each quarter.

It is intended that the Visiting Committee shall thus become intimately acquainted with church affairs in its own district; shall give notice to the Pastor at once of any case of sickness, or other special call for his services, and carry a welcome to new families which may arrive from time to time.

Usually it is so arranged that the districts do not number more than twelve to fifteen families each, but the Pulaskiville and Somerville districts, need special provision. In the latter case the Visiting Committee has been enlarged by the addition of a company of young church-members, living within the district, who have rendered most efficient service, calling upon the sick, upon the new arrivals at the chapel, etc. Throughout the congregation, several hundred calls are thus made every year, and though the results may not be immediately evident in every case, yet they are well worth any effort which they have cost. A tract is left at each visit, and valuable religious help has been given and received during these calls; but much is gained, even when, as in so many cases, the conversation is simply that of informal neighborly kindness.

The Standing Committee on Social Receptions.

At least twice each year the congregation is expected to spend an evening together, purely for social intercourse. These receptions are held in the early Summer, and in the Fall; that is to say, just before the people are scattered, more or less, for the vacation season, and also when the cool weather brings the season for renewing active work. Whatever special occasions may offer, are also used in the same way. The Sunday-school room, which is very large, and was originally planned so as to serve this purpose when desired, is the place of meeting. Sometimes there are refreshments, sometimes not. There is never any elaborate programme, for the one object is simply to introduce new members to the older ones, and to enable each to take by the hand as many others as possible. The Committee consists of a few members of experience, who are aided by the young ladies at large. Sub-committees are arranged for decorating the rooms, for receiving the guests as they enter, etc.

The Standing Committee on Furnishing the Church Building.

This Committee was of sufficient importance, and existed sufficiently long, to be added to the list of the Society, though it was discontinued with the final accomplishment of its work. Very efficient service was rendered, both in securing the requisite amount of funds, and in supervising the furnishing of the new church building in 1872.

THE STANDING COMMITTEE ON CARE OF THE CHURCH BUILDING.

This is a Committee of experienced houskeepers, who give to carpets and cushions, walls and floors, the benefit of their supervision. They have rendered valuable assistance in securing faithful work from various employés, and especially in the various house-cleanings, of which all public edifices are at times in need.

THE STANDING COMMITTEE ON FLOWERS FOR CHURCH SERVICES.

The object of this Committee, is to keep a list of those persons in the congregation, who offer to send flowers for the pulpit; and to arrange with them the various details of the matter, so that each may have his own turn, and as many as possible be enlisted for contributing.

THE STANDING COMMITTEE ON LADIES' PRAYER-MEETINGS.

Since the winter of 1873–74, a weekly prayer-meeting has, with occasional interruptions, been continued by the ladies of this Society. At first it was held at the church, in the afternoon of the day on which the Mother's Meeting was held, and just after that meeting. For two or three years, meetings for the younger ladies were also held on Sunday evening, before service, in the Ladies' room; these were often attended by thirty-five or forty persons, and were full of spiritual interest. Those who were most active in them were reluctantly obliged, however, to discontinue them, because of inability to attend them in addition to the fatiguing mission work and other services of the day. This particular hour was sometimes the only one in the day, which was available for quiet meditation and prayer at home. The afternoon meeting was also discontinued for one season, but was then resumed, with more energy than before. This was in the Fall of 1877, and both time and place were changed; a morning hour was chosen, and the meeting was in charge of the pastor's wife, at her own home. The only change which has since been made was that of the place, back again to the church, to suit the convenience of some among the increasing number of attendants. Very marked interest has been manifested in these services of prayer and conference; those who have attended once, have usually tried to come again. The good results are unmistakable, and it is hoped that this gathering will remain not only a permanent, but an increasingly prominent feature of our church life.

The Standing Committee on Sewing Circle.

It may appear strange that the old-fashioned Sewing Circle should have so little prominence, among such a list of organizations; yet it only illustrates again, the fact that every congregation has its own individuality, and that any Society like this must be elastic enough to adapt itself to that individuality, and even to its changes from one year to another. In 1875-76, such meetings were held at the various houses of the members, and in 1877-78, at the Pastor's Study in the church. In each case the ladies met at four o'clock, and had tea from six to seven; the gentlemen, and those members who were unable to attend earlier, coming in the evening. The Committee continues its organization, and doubtless will find room for activity again in future seasons.

THE STANDING COMMITTEE ON PARISH LIBRARY.

This Committee was formed in November, 1878, and members of the congregation were invited to bring books for the nucleus of a Library, at the Social Reception held in that month. More than two hundred volumes are on hand, and ready for use on Wednesday evenings after the service, the books being kept in the room immediately adjoining the Lecture Room. There can be little doubt of the usefulness of such a Library, especially when it reaches a more satisfactory size.

THE PASTORAL AID SOCIETY

had collected and expended, through these various committees, at the time of its Ninth Annual Report, in April, 1879, the following amounts:

FOR EXTERNAL MISSION WORK.

Home Missions,	$6,122 66
Foreign Missions,	5,000 58
	$11,123 24

FOR NEIGHBORHOOD MISSION WORK.

Pulaskiville Sunday-school (Building and Work),	$3,710 70
Somerville Sunday-school (Building and Work),	5,152 18
Relief of the Poor,	2,943 55
Bible-reader's Work,	2,035 33
Dorcas Work,	561 21
Mother's Meetings,	234 57
Tracts,	67 04
Benevolent Institutions,	1,456 05
	$16,160 63

FOR CONGREGATIONAL PURPOSES.

Receptions, Church Furnishing, etc.,	$ 1,087 00
Total,	$28,370 87

The remaining part of our church work is largely of such a nature, as to be carried on by the usual organizations, comprising both sexes; such as the Sunday-Schools, the choir (which is always composed of church members), etc.

Although there is no single society of the male members, on such a scale as the Pastoral Aid Society, yet it of course devolves upon them to act as officers of the schools, etc.; and all the church operations are supervised by those who constitute the Session and Board of Trustees. Besides this, there have been organizations of Young Men for various objects, e. g., for holding prayer meetings of their own, on Sabbath evenings, as early as 1870; for extending the hospitality of the church to visitors; for co-operating with the Young Men's Christian Association of Germantown; and especially for conducting prayer meetings, and otherwise carrying on gospel work at Pulaskiville. Further reference to this will be made on another page. For the last two years a Young Men's Society has existed, whose object is primarily the holding of social meetings each month, at which lectures, illustrated in various ways, concerts, etc., are given. Even at the first of these meetings there were fifty of our young men present, and they have continued to be successful and beneficial. There is in this the germ of much larger fruitfulness in the future.

THE SUNDAY-SCHOOL WORK is one which has formed a marked feature of our church life, almost from the very beginning. As early as April 25th, 1819, a school was formed, "for instructing the children to read, and learn by heart, portions of scripture." It attracted children from all parts of the village; so that, although the community was still distinctively German, there were as many as 300 children present. The other churches, however, soon made provision for their own children, so that this school depended for support mainly upon the families of the congregation itself. It is now closing its sixty-first year, with fresh tokens of life and usefulness.

The ordinary business of the school is carried on by a "Sabbath-School Association," which was formed for the purpose many years ago. This is by no means an independent or irresponsible body; but one which maintains the closest relations with the Church Session. For example, the preamble to its Constitution reads as follows: "We the undersigned, Sabbath-School officers and teachers, having associated ourselves together in order to accomplish more effectively the great work committed to our charge, do adopt for our government the following Constitution: the same, together with all proceedings under it, being subject always to the approval of the church Session." Then follow articles by which the Pastor is recognized as ex-officio President of the Association: teachers are appointed by the Superintendent, with the approval of the Session, etc. The General Assembly, and the Westminster Standards, declare explicitly the responsibility, and therefore the authority of the Session, in regard to all church work; and this principle is recognized practically by all our organizations. Experience has shown that our loyalty to the standards on this point, has always been of great service in securing not only harmony, but efficiency.

In 1879, there were 420 names enrolled in connection with the school; so that its membership is not far from that of the two Mission schools taken together. The three schools are closely connected in various ways: and a goodly proportion of our church membership may be found in them as active workers. The interest of the congregation at large, is manifested in subscriptions for the various school expenses, and in the large attendance upon any special occasions in the school life. The two Mission School Anniversaries, which follow each other in October, the three Christmas Festivals, which fill the holiday week so pleasantly from year to year, and especially the Anniversary of the Home School every Spring, are never lacking in crowds of eagerly interested attendants. At the Spring Anniversary, indeed, when all three schools are present, the church building has for some years been wholly unable to furnish even standing room, for those who desire to be present. The children occupy most of the seats, and the aisles are filled with visitors who remain, though obliged to stand for hours, until the closing exercises. The Sabbath-School choir have become, under the faithful training of the School organist, and led by the cornets, a most efficient help, not only on these public occasions, but in the ordinary sessions from week to week. Of course the real power of the School for the conversion and training of its children, is found in faithful, personal effort, under the guidance of the Great Teacher.

In the two chapels, Sabbath-School work is connected various other forms of mission enterprise. At Pulaski-ville, weekly prayer meetings have been held since January, 1871; just after the chapel was erected. These were at first in charge of the various elders, who served in rotation: and were held on Tuesday evenings, but afterward on Friday. In September, 1871, they were given by the Session into the hands of Dr. Geo. H. Burgin, who changed the time for holding them to Sabbath evening. In this form, they were attended with much success, until the sad interruption which was caused by Dr. Burgin's sickness and death, in January, 1873. The devotedness and efficiency of his work will not soon be forgotten.

In the next month, February, 1873, the Rev. Mr. Travis, who was at the time acting as Principal of the Germantown Academy, and in attendance at this Church, took up the work, and continued in charge of it until late in the Fall, when other duties compelled him to resign it.

Early in January, 1874, some of the young men in the Church began to hold regular meetings at a private house near the chapel; and iu the following summer, the people of the neighborhood came together more largely than at any previous time, in attendance upon such services. It became necessary to return to the chapel in order to find room enough; and since September, 1874, the meetings have continued to be held there.

In January, 1876, Mr. William Johnson was called in, with the hope that his attractive singing might bring within reach of the gospel yet larger numbers. He was present on four occasions, and during that season many meetings were held by the young men, and by the other members of the church in this neighborhood. The attendance was sometimes more than one hundred and fifty at these services, and for a long time afterward additional meetings were held from house to house on Thursdays, with an average attendance of about thirty. Many additions were made to the church at the communion, three months afterward, and the work resulted in much permanent good. This meeting is still in charge of the young men of the church, and continues to be a valuable feature of our mission work. The chapel has also been used for Gospel Temperance meetings and other services. The daily Parish School, Sewing School, etc., held there for some years, have already been described. This little building has proved to be a spring of wholesome influences in all the neighborhood, and its work has re-acted in the most beneficial manner upon the church itself.

The chapel which we erected for our Somerville Mission School, has also been used for devotional services in the evening. The difficulty of procuring enough lay helpers for this purpose, in a place so remote from the main body of the congregation, led to the suggestion that a fund be raised sufficient to provide salary for a minister, who might take charge of the proposed services. This plan was therefore brought before Session, by those of our people who were especially interested in that field ; together with the statement that the condition of affairs was still such, as to manifestly preclude any thought of forming a new organization there for years to come ; and that the success of the work depended wholly upon its being recognized by all our members as their own enterprise, under the direct charge of their own Pastor and Session, and for which they as a church had the entire responsibility. This was so evidently the case, that even while the Session continued to hope that this mission might ultimately become itself a church, they concurred in the belief that for the present, and indeed until the condition of the field should materially alter in a way of which no signs had yet appeared, it must be kept before this congregation as an integral part of our own parish work.   -

The title of "Chapel Minister" has been given by the General Assembly to those whom a Session may entrust with such services, in a mission station under its care. The first to occupy in this way the pulpit of our Somerville Chapel was the Rev. Mr. Hofford, then of Doylestown, Penna., who preached on Sabbath evenings for some three months, his salary being provided by the church in the form of private subscriptions. Other engagements, however, prevented him from entering upon the work as fully as he at first intended, and caused him to relinquish it. In January, 1877, another Chapel Minister was therefore engaged, viz.: the Rev. Mosely H. Williams. As the work was no longer a mere experiment, regular annual subscribers were now secured, so as to provide for the minister's salary in this way as far as possible, and avoid the necessity of special collections.

The wish for a weekly prayer-meeting in the chapel was now gratified, since the residence of Mr. Williams in the part of Germantown toward Somerville enabled him to inaugurate services of this kind. This was done at his own suggestion, and is indicative of his cordial interest in the work. Both meetings were well attended and successful. In the Fall of 1878, it was believed that the way was open for still further enlargement of the work, and application was made, by the members connected with this part of our church work, for arrangements whereby two services might be held each Sabbath, and regular visiting be carried on throughout the week. After some time had been spent in considering this application, and ascertaining the condition of the field itself, the session agreed to sanction it, and provision was made for securing additional funds in order to bring up the salary to the requisite amount.

The Rev. Mr. Williams was precluded by other engagements from accepting the position in its enlarged form, and after conference with several other brethren, an agreement was finally made with the Rev. James W. Kirk, who became our Chapel Minister, March 19th, 1879. Good results from this enlargement of the work were shown immediately, and this whole wing of the church force is now equipped for excellent service.

Some of the other features of church life during the last decade may be grouped together as follows.

In connection with our Sabbath worship it is to be noted that the afternoon service was transferred to evening in the Spring of 1870 : this change, together with that of the weekly prayer meeting from Friday to Wednesday, being in the direction of harmony with the other churches in the vicinity, and attended with good results.

The Sabbath morning service has been introduced by the Doxology, since June, 1870 ; and it is especially note-

worthy that since June, 1873, every service, during the
week, or on the Lord's Day, has been closed, not merely
with the Benediction, but with a pause for silent prayer.
Before pronouncing the Benediction, and also immediately
after it, the congregation stands in entire silence, long
enough to give opportunity for such prayer, and therefore
to secure a reverential conclusion to the worship of God.
This suggestion was accepted at once, when first proposed,
and has never needed to be renewed.

During the present pastorate, persons received into
communion upon profession of faith, have been given a
public welcome, before partaking of the Lord's Supper.
The form used for this purpose will be found at the close
of this book. It will be noticed that these persons are
presented to the congregation, not as candidates for
reception, but as already in full membership, and to be
welcomed as such.

The Week of Prayer has been observed, at the beginning
of each year; and the following programme, with slight
verbal alterations, has been in use, almost from the com-
mencement of this pastorate:

Sabbath. The petition, "Thy Kingdom Come:" and,
in order to the fulfillment of this, prayer for the out-
pouring of the Holy Spirit upon all flesh.

Monday. Thanksgiving for that which God has done to
bring the world to Himself, and confession of our short-
coming as fellow-laborers with Him.

Tuesday. Prayer for the out-pouring of the Holy Spirit
upon THE FAMILY, and its supplementary agencies the
Sunday Schools, Colleges, etc., in all lands.

Wednesday. Prayer for the out-pouring of the Holy
Spirit upon THE NATIONS, and for political and social
reform, temperance, etc.

Thursday. For the out-pouring of the Holy Spirit upon THE CHURCH UNIVERSAL, in its ministry and membership.

Friday. For the out-pouring of the Holy Spirit upon THE CHURCH IN ITS FOREIGN MISSION WORK, and for the conversion of the heathen.

Saturday. Prayer for the out-pouring of the Holy Spirit upon THE CHURCH IN ITS HOME MISSIONS, and for the conversion of souls in our own land, especially in the locality where the prayer-meeting is held.

It was intended to secure for our Church, by the use of this programme, certain advantages which were often lacking in the schedule prepared by the Evangelical Alliance. *e. g.* The same prominence is given to the coming of the Holy Spirit, and to the Kingdom of Christ in all the earth, which characterized the prayer-meetings during the days before Pentecost. This was the model after which the Week of Prayer was originally formed, in the year 1860: but in the course of time it was greatly changed, even to the omitting, or the barely mentioning of the Holy Spirit in some of the programmes.

Again: it was by Foreign Missionaries that this Week was originated, and with the express object of securing universal prayer for the world-wide interests of Christianity: but we sometimes found the whole week passing away with no distinct emphasis whatever upon Foreign Missions. In our programme, the last two days are assigned, the one to Foreign and the other to Home Missions; and on all the other days, both the universal and the local references are included.

Another advantage sought, was the more orderly arrangement of topics for prayer. In the published schedules, these were often unduly multiplied, and grouped in the most incongruous manner; whereas they might all be classified with the Family, the Nation, or the Church, the three Divine institutions for reaching men.

We were frequently urged, in view of such facts, to disregard the usual programmes entirely, and confine the week altogether to prayer for a local revival: but it seemed better to act on the plan above indicated, in the expectation that it would help and not hinder us, in seeking for success in our own work.

We are confirmed in this judgment by the fact that within the last two years this programme has been adopted, substantially, in several different cities, by those to whom it has been made known; and also by the Synod of Philadelphia.

There have been several seasons of marked religious interest during this period. In 1870, it was to such a time of special quickening, that the project of building a new edifice owed its first impulse. The entrance into this building in 1872, was followed by another experience of the same kind.

In the Spring and Summer of 1874, there was a manifest desire for special meetings, quite a number of which were held, with large attendance and good results. Still later, we shared in the benefits accruing to many of the neighboring churches in the Winter and Spring of 1876, from the prominence given to religious subjects by the public at . large, in connection with the Moody and Sankey meetings in Philadelphia. Only one person, indeed, of the sixty who were that year added to this church by profession of faith, traced his conversion directly to these meetings: but they greatly aided in maintaining a religious atmosphere favorable to such results. One marked feature during all these periods, has been the increase of the spirit of united prayer, as shown, not only in the enlarged attendance and deeper interest of the congregational prayer-meeting, but

in special meetings held among themselves by the young
men, and others by the young women and girls: the
Ladies' Prayer-Meeting described in connection with the
Pastoral Aid Society, is another instance of the same kind.
It is pleasant to note the fact, that two of our members
have been ordained within this period to the gospel
ministry: Revs. Alexander Henry and George Yeisley.
The former will be especially remembered, as born and
nurtured within the congregation.

The Session of the church has had several changes of
membership. In 1870 the elders were T. Charlton Henry,
Joseph W. Parks, and Enoch Taylor. In January, 1871,
William Adamson and Thomas MacKellar were added; in
December, 1874, Edward L. Wilson, and in December,
1876, Charles M. Lukens. Elders Parks and Adamson
afterward removed, the former to another part of the
country, and the latter to the Wakefield Church, in whose
session he remained until his death (in 1879).

The formation of the Sessional Union may be taken as
indicative of our fraternal relation toward the neighboring
churches. As early as October, 1870, this Session extended
an invitation to the others in Germantown, looking toward
such a Union: some unexpected difficulties were encountered at that time, but information of their removal was
received in June, 1872, and the invitation, being then
renewed, was at once accepted. All the active members
of every session in Germantown were enrolled, and a
permanent organization was formed; its object being
" fraternal consultation and united action upon those
subjects in which our churches have a common interest."
The meetings of this Union have continued to be most
pleasant and profitable, both in the promotion of brotherly
feeling, and in efficient action upon various matters of
importance.

One of its first fruits was the organization of the Wake-field Presbyterian Church of Germantown. Early in the year 1873 Elder Wm. Adamson informed his fellow-elders in this church, that he had, for a long time felt the call to secure a new Presbyterian Church in the lower part of the town, where a large field existed, unoccupied by any congregation, and becoming rapidly populated; and that he now felt himself able to undertake this enterprise, in view of the fact that our own people were fully settled in their new edifice, and could afford to dismiss him. The Session at once expressed hearty sympathy with him in this plan, and although deeply regretting the separation from us which it involved, pledged him its cordial support. The matter was then laid before the Sessional Union: Mr. Adamson offering to give a lot valued at $9000 for the new church, and agreeing to commence building at once, in case the three congregations should subscribe as much as $3000 in all, toward the fund. Considerably more than this sum was at once pledged. In a letter written by Mr. Adamson · some time afterward, he stated to us that $4107.65 had been received from the three congregations, of which sum $2013.95, or nearly one-half, had come from that of the First Church. Upon the receipt of his letter, this Session sent him an additional sum, bringing our total contribution for the Building Fund up to $2100, which was the amount we had expected to raise, although no promise to that effect had ever been given. This action was taken "as an expression of fraternal regard for Bro. Adamson, and with hearty desire for the still more abundant success of the new church." Toward this, our youngest sister-church, there still exists the same cordial sympathy, which led us then to open the way for the unobstructed departure of so cherished an elder as Mr. Adamson, and of any other members who inclined to follow his example. The subscriptions which have lately been given by members of this congregation, toward the proposed erection of another and larger edifice for the Wakefield Church, are but further indications of the same spirit. Toward the other two churches, the same disposition of warm fraternal regard has always been ready to show itself. The visit paid to us by the Market Square Church, during the work of repairing its own edifice in September and October, 1872, is still most pleasurably remembered. A similar invitation was afterward extended to the Second Church under the same circumstances, and with the same motive.

As would naturally be expected, the Young Men's Christian Association of Germantown has received support and aid from this church, since its first organization. It traces its foundation chiefly to the christian zeal of Mr. Adamson, who was at that time, and for some years afterward, still in this church. He did not content himself with the efficient work he was doing here, however, but sought to influence the whole community for good. His personal efforts, and the responsibility for its current expenses, which he so long carried, were indispensable to its success. In this he was sustained by the other members of the church. The Board of Trustees put $3000 into the Young Men's Christian Association Stock, and others gave enough to make a total contribution, amounting to one-half of all the unconditional subscriptions received from every source, when the building was occupied. The Association held its public meetings in this church, until, through Mr. Adamson's advancing a large part of the necessary sum, it purchased our former edifice and remodeled it for its own uses.

Toward all its sister churches of every denomination, and toward all christian work, this church has ever been glad to manifest the spirit of brotherly co-operation. For example, the Convention which carried on the Germantown Local Option movement, held its meetings in our building, and chose for its President one of our elders, Mr. Thomas MacKellar ; and other enterprises which require united Christian support, appeal continually with confidence and success to the sympathy of this people.

There are, of course, other features in the church life and work which might be mentioned, but enough has been given to indicate its general character and tendency.

Such a review is the more appropriate at this particular time, because the Pastor has felt himself led, in the Providence of God, to take measures for resigning his charge at the beginning of the new year (1880). The collection and arrangement of the various facts which are here included, has been to him a labor of love. It is meant to be, on his part, a token of hearty appreciation for the unceasing affection and cordiality, with which the people of this beloved church have continually surrounded him.

It is also hoped that each of the members, into whose hands this little book may come, will accept it as a personal appeal to himself, to enter into his own share in the common work, with fresh zeal and consecration. "Lift up your eyes and look on the fields, for they are white already to harvest ; and he that reapeth receiveth wages, and gathereth fruit, unto life eternal."

FORMS OF WORSHIP.

[*As connected with the history of this Church, a copy is herewith given, of the forms which have been used in its public worship.*]

The usual Order of Services on the Sabbath, has been as follows:

MORNING WORSHIP.

Doxology.   [Congregation rising.]
Brief Invocation.   [Congregation still standing.]
Hymn.
Decalogue, or other Scripture Lesson.
   [Anthem, if any.]
Notices.
   [Collection, if any.]
Prayer.
Hymn.
Sermon.
Prayer.
Hymn.   [Congregation rising.]
Benediction.   [Preceded and followed by silent prayer.]

EVENING WORSHIP.

Anthem.
Scripture-lesson.
Hymn.
Prayer.
Hymn.
Sermon.
Prayer.
Hymn.   [Congregation rising.]
Benediction [and silent prayer, as at every service.]

BAPTISM.—Baptism has usually been administered to children, after the first hymn and before the Scripture-lesson, at the Morning Service, as follows:

Reading of Mark x. 13–17. [Parents enter and are seated.]
Address [during which the parents arise.]
Prayer ;—Baptism ;—Prayer :
Hymn.

THE LORD'S SUPPER.—On Communion Day, the following order has been observed :

Doxology.
Invocation.
Hymn.
Scripture-lesson.
Notices.
Collection for Poor Fund.
Announcement and Recognition of New Members.
Brief Address or Sermon.
Invitation to the Lord's Supper.
Hymn.
[At the Communion-table.]
Prayer.
Distribution of Bread [in silence.]
Prayer.
Distribution of Wine [in silence.]
Hymn.
Benediction [and silent prayer.]

PUBLIC RECOGNITION TO CHURCH MEMBERS.

[By the Presbyterian Constitution, the question of admitting any person into church membership is entrusted solely and entirely to the Session, which consists of the Pastor and Ruling Elders.

It is by the act of the Session, and not by that of any public assembly of the whole congregation, that admittance is given. In the case of unbaptized persons, however, it is required that after being thus accepted by the Session, they shall repeat their confession of faith in Christ publicly, and thereupon be baptized. In the case of those who were "born within the pale of the visible Church," and have been recognized as such by Baptism in childhood, no public act is necessary in order to their entrance upon full Communion, beyond a confession of their faith in Christ, made in the presence of the Session. Nevertheless it is allowable to give them the privilege of repeating this confession before the whole church, and thus receiving its public welcome and recognition.

It is to be remembered, therefore, that such persons do not stand before the congregation as candidates, who are then and there to be given admittance into church membership: but that they are already in full membership, and are to be welcomed as such.

And with regard to this confession itself, it is carefully to be noted, that all which can be required of any person, before admitting him into Communion, is that he trust and obey Christ, and seek the peace and welfare of the Church. In the words which have expressed the rule of our Church on this matter since the year 1729: "We are willing to admit to fellowship in sacred ordinances, all such as we have ground to believe Christ will at last admit to the kingdom of heaven."

There is a most important difference between the requirement which is made upon private members, and that which is made upon public officers. The Church as an organization, does hold faithfully to the system of doctrine which is contained in the Westminster Standards: and before any person is given authority to represent the Church by holding one of its public offices, he must be able to declare that he in person does sincerely and unfeignedly accept and believe that system as true. One who undertakes to publicly teach in the name of the Church, must of course be required to teach nothing which is contrary to its creed. But private members are considered to be learners, rather than teachers. All which is asked concerning their religious opinions is, that they be such as not to interfere with trusting and obeying Christ, as their God and Saviour, or with seeking the peace and welfare of the Church.

It is upon these cherished principles of our beloved Church, which combine faithfulness to the truth, with the utmost broadness of Christian liberality, that the following service is formed.]

Form of Public Recognition.

"The following announcement is made by the Session of this church:

We have received by Certificate [A. from church of B.], whom we commend to you, as henceforth your fellow-members.

We have agreed that [C. and D.] shall be admitted into the church by Baptism, after publicly repeating the Confession of Faith, which [they] made in our presence.

We have admitted to the Lord's Table [E. and F.], who, being already baptized as children of the church, are now advanced into its full communion, upon Confession of Faith. This Confession will now be repeated before you, in order that public recognition and welcome may be given by the whole church.

[They will now arise:]

Dearly Beloved: Remember the words of the Lord Jesus, how He said, "Whosoever shall confess me before men, him shall the Son of Man also confess, before the angels of God." In the presence therefore of men, and of angels, and of the heart-searching God, do you solemnly confess and declare that you believe in the Lord Jesus Christ, as your God and Saviour?

Consider what it is to believe in Christ; so that you may the better hold fast the profession of your faith without wavering.

The Lord Jesus hath graciously promised to give Himself, in all His saving power and love, unto every soul which will accept Him. If we believe, or have faith, in Him, we will thus accept Him; we will entrust ourselves unto Him to be saved; and rely upon Him alone, for everlasting life. Day by day, therefore, will we go unto Him for every needful blessing, but especially for pardon, and for strength against sin. Moreover, we will show our faith in Him by endeavoring, in this Divine strength, to follow and obey the Lord in all things.

Is it with this meaning and purpose, that you now make confession of your faith?

Furthermore; if you receive Christ as your Lord, you will accept His people to be your people: entering into covenant with us to seek the peace and welfare of His Church, and faithfully to perform your part in its work and worship, so far as Christ may enable you.

Is this also your desire and purpose?

[IN CASE OF BAPTISM.]

[The sign and seal of this covenant with the Lord, and of membership in His Church, is to be given by the administration of Baptism, whenever, as at this time, we receive any person who is not already baptized. The water which is used signifies the cleansing power of Christ's blood, applied by the Holy Ghost; and the words which are spoken, signify the bringing of the soul which is thus cleansed, into the Baptism, or under the complete influence, of Father, Son, and Holy Ghost, which is life everlasting.

This Ordinance will now be administered.

(Prayer;—Baptism;—Prayer.)]

[*The members of this church will now arise.*] We therefore, as members of this church, do give you hearty welcome in the name of the Lord Jesus, to sit down with us at His table. We accept your covenant with us, and engage on our part to treat you in love, as members of the Body of Christ; aiding you on the journey toward heaven, as God may give us opportunity.

It behooves us all to remember, that these covenant obligations to Christ and to one another, are already enjoined upon us by the Lord Himself, as our solemn duty, from which we have no right to withhold our consent. Let us therefore pray without ceasing, for that grace through which alone we shall keep them faithfully. Let us thank Him for permitting us to become fellow-laborers with God, and with one another. And when our communion of labor and of love with the church on earth is dissolved, may God receive us all into fellowship with the Church Triumphant in heaven, through Jesus Christ our Lord, to whom be glory forever: Amen.

> Blest be the tie that binds
>   Our hearts in Christian love;
> The fellowship of kindred minds
>   Is like to that above.
>
> Before our Father's throne,
>   We pour our ardent prayers;
> Our fears, our hopes, our aims are one,
>   Our comforts and our cares.

[*To be sung as closing this part of the Service.*]

INVITATION TO THE LORD'S SUPPER.

And now, before we enter upon the Communion Service, let us read that which is written concerning this Holy Supper, in the First Epistle to the Corinthians, at the eleventh chapter.

"For I have received of the Lord that which also I delivered unto you, That the Lord Jesus, the same night in which He was betrayed, took bread: And when He had given thanks, He brake it, and said, Take, eat: this is my body which is broken for you: this do in remembrance of me. After the same manner also He took the cup, when He had supped, saying, This cup is the new covenant in my blood: this do ye, as oft as ye drink it, in remembrance of me. For as often as ye eat this bread, and drink this cup, ye do shew the Lord's death, till He come."

The Lord's Supper is the ordinance of Jesus Christ Himself. Until He come again, His people are to eat this bread and drink this cup in remembrance of Him. It is therefore in obedience to the express commandment of our Lord, that we come now to His table.

And I remind you, in the words of our Church, "that it is of inestimable benefit, to strengthen Christ's people against sin; to support them under troubles; to encourage and quicken them in duty; to inspire them with love and zeal; to increase their faith and holy resolution; and to beget peace of conscience, and comfortable hopes of eternal life."

I am also charged to give warning, that the profane, the ignorant and scandalous, and those who are wilfully purposed in their hearts to continue indulging themselves in any known sin, are not to approach this holy table.

On the other hand, I am to invite unto it, those of you who are sensible of your lost and helpless state by sin, and who therefore depend upon the atonement of Christ for pardon and acceptance with God: who are sufficiently instructed in Gospel truth to understand the meaning and use of this ordinance, and who desire to renounce their sins, being determined by Christ's grace to lead a holy life, in love toward God, with peace and charity toward men; "forgiving one another, even as God for Christ's sake hath forgiven you."

I therefore, cordially invite all such as are here described, and especially, if they are strangers and visitors from other churches, to partake with us. It is the table of the Lord, and not ours; whomsoever the Spirit of the Lord invites, let not man hinder from coming.

Neither let us be discouraged because of the sins and imperfections which yet remain within us, even against our wills, but remember His own most gracious word,

"Come unto me, all ye that labor and are heavy-laden, and I will give you rest."

"They that are whole need not a physician, but they that are sick; I came, not to call the righteous, but sinners to repentance."

"Behold, I stand at the door and knock; if any man hear my voice and open the door, I will come in to him, and sup with him, and he with me."

WORDS USED IN THE LORD'S SUPPER.

Dearly Beloved: The Lord Jesus began this holy supper with prayer and thanksgiving; after His example, therefore, let us pray. [*Prayer.*]

And now let us obey the Lord Jesus, who, the same night in which He was betrayed, took bread, and when He had given thanks, He brake it, and said: "Take, eat, this is my body, which is broken for you: this do in remembrance of me." [*Distribution of Bread.*]

It is written that, "after the same manner also," He

took the cup; that is, after He had again looked up to
God in prayer and thanksgiving. According to His
example let us again unite in prayer. [*Prayer.*]

As it is written, then, "He took the cup, and when He
had given thanks, He gave it unto them, saying, This cup
is the new covenant in my blood; this do ye, as oft as ye
drink it, in remembrance of me." [*Distribution of Wine.*]

And finally, it is written, that "when they had sung an
hymn, they went out;" let us also, therefore, close our
communion service with a hymn.

FORM FOR BAPTISM OF INFANTS.

[Doxology. Invocation. Hymn. Read Mark x: 13-16.]
Opportunity is now to be given for the Baptism of
Children.   .

We administer unto them this ordinance, because we
accept it as the will of Christ, that children of believers
are still to be recognized as children of the Church, even
as they were under the Old Testament; and that Baptism
is the form appointed by Him for this purpose. The water
which is used, signifies the cleansing power of Christ's
blood, applied by the Holy Ghost; and the words which
are spoken, signify the bringing of the soul which is thus
cleansed, into the Baptism, or under the complete
influence, of Father, Son, and Holy Ghost, which is life
everlasting. This outward sign is given by the Lord Jesus
Christ, as the token and seal of a covenant between Himself
and the believing parents; a covenant whereby He doth
engage to provide, and they to use, His Divine grace and
guidance for themselves and their children; so that, if
they do not receive these everlasting blessings of His
kingdom, it will be from no lack of faithfulness on His
part.

The parents, who desire thus to present their children for Baptism, will show the same by rising.

Beloved in the Lord; consider what is your part in that solemn covenant with God, which you are now to seal.

It implies that you confess the need of a Divine cleansing for us all, seeing we are by nature sinful, guilty and polluted: that you look for this cleansing unto the Lord Jesus Christ, and accept Him to be Saviour and King unto yourselves and your children; that you engage to teach them His will, as it is written in the Holy Scriptures; [and for a summary of this, we recommend to you the Catechism of the Church;] that you will pray with them, and for them; setting them an example of piety and godliness, and endeavoring by all the means of God's appointment, to bring them up in the nurture and. admonition of the Lord.

Is it your desire now to seal this covenant, and to keep it faithfully hereafter by God's grace?

[Prayer: Baptism: Prayer: Hymn.]

MARRIAGE FORMULA.

God be merciful unto us, and bless us, and cause His face to shine upon us.

Dearly Beloved : Let us have the comfortable assurance that the Lord our God is willing, most graciously to have regard unto those who come before Him to be united in marriage. For it was by God our Creator, that this holy estate of matrimony was established, when Himself united in marriage our first parents, in all the purity and innocence of the garden of Eden. It was confirmed by the gracious presence and miraculous blessing of God our Saviour at the wedding in Cana. And God the Holy Ghost hath declared it honorable in all, and made it a symbol of the union between Christ and His Church.

Wherefore since marriage is in itself a holy thing, and well pleasing in the sight of God the Father, Son, and Holy Ghost, you ought with all confidence and strong desire to look unto Him for His sanction and blessing.

Let us Pray.

Most gracious God our heavenly Father, we beseech Thee for these, Thy son and daughter, that they may, with reverent trust in Thee, enter into this covenant of marriage. Look upon them with Thy favor and blessing: and do Thou bear witness to their vows, which are made not only to each other but to Thee. Grant this, oh Father, with the forgiveness of our sins, through Jesus Christ, Thy Son. Amen.

In further token of your desire and purpose, let each of you now take the other by the right hand.

[To the Man.]

Do you, [A.] take her whom you now hold by the hand, before God and these witnesses, to be your wife? Do you promise to love her, honor her, defend her, sustain and cherish, her in joy and in sorrow, in health and in sickness, in prosperity and in adversity; to be faithful to her in all things, as becometh a good husband, and never forsake her, so long as you both do live?

[I do.]

[To the Woman.]

Do you, [B.] take him whom you now hold by the hand, before God and these witnesses, to be your husband? Do you promise to love him, honor him, cherish and obey him, in joy and in sorrow, in health and in sickness, in prosperity and in adversity; to be faithful to him in all things, as becometh a good wife, and never forsake him so long as you both do live?

[I do.]

[*In case a Ring is to be used.*]

You have signified your desire to use a Ring, as the visible sign and seal of your marriage. Do you therefore now give this Ring in token that you will truly perform these your vows?

[I do.]

Do you receive this Ring in token of the same on your part?

[I do.]

Let each again take the other by the right hand.]

Now, therefore, in the name of the Father, Son, and Holy Ghost, I pronounce you husband and wife.

What God hath joined together, let not man put asunder.

Let us Pray.

O God, our heavenly Father, grant unto these Thy children grace, that they may faithfully keep this vow and covenant which they have now made, and steadfastly abide in holy love, to each other and to Thee. Shine upon them with the fulness of Thy Divine love. And above all, as Thou hast made these twain to become one flesh, grant them also that one Spirit, by Whose grace they may each be united unto Christ, Thy Son ; that this union one to another, may be in the Lord, and may cause them the better to serve Thee and rejoice in Thee, not only in this world, but in that which is to come, through Jesus Christ, Thy Son.   Amen.

The Lord bless you and keep you ; the Lord make His face to shine upon you, and be gracious unto you ; the Lord lift up His countenance upon you, and give you peace !

CONSTITUTION AND BY-LAWS

OF THE

PASTORAL AID SOCIETY.

CONSTITUTION.

I.—Name.

This Association shall be known as the Pastoral Aid Society of the First Presbyterian Church in Germantown.

II.—Objects.

Its general object shall be, to organize the ladies of the congregation for Christian usefulness.

Its specific objects and plans shall be determined, from time to time, by agreement between the Society and the Session.

III.—Membership.

Any lady connected with the Church or congregation may become a member of this Society, on signing its constitution; by which act it is understood that she pledges herself to observe its regulations, and to aid in its active work, unless prevented by higher duties.

IV.—Organization.

1. The officers of the Society shall consist of a President, Vice President, Secretary, and Treasurer.

2. The work of the Society shall be performed by means of Standing Committees, each having charge of its own specific object.

3. There shall be an Executive Committee, consisting of the President and Secretary, with three other members. It shall have general supervision of the Society's work, and shall agree with the Session upon the above-named

"specific objects" of effort. It shall have power to call special meetings of the Society, to transfer members from one Standing Committee to another, and to form new Standing Committees, at the desire or with the consent of the members immediately interested. It shall itself have membership *ex officio* in every Standing Committee, and in all its proceedings shall be subject to correction by a vote of the Society.

V.—MEETINGS.

1. The Society shall hold a regular meeting within the first week of April, June, October, December and February.

2. At the April meeting, the Secretary and Treasurer shall present their annual reports; and there shall be held an election of Officers and Executive Committee for the ensuing year.

3. Ten members shall constitute a quorum for the transaction of business at any meeting.

4. After each regular meeting, the Secretary shall cause the minute-book to be laid before the Church Session.

VI.—AMENDMENTS.

Amendments to this constitution may be proposed at any regular meeting, but the vote thereon shall not be taken until the ensuing regular meeting, and the consent of two-thirds of those present shall be required for their adoption.

BY-LAWS.

I.—Standing Committees and Their Duties.

The Standing Committees shall be as follows:

MISSIONARY WORK.

1. On Domestic Missions: to continue the work of the Domestic Missionary Society founded in 1852. (See Appendix to By-Laws, 1.)

2. On Foreign Missions: to aid in Woman's Work for Woman.

NEIGHBORHOOD WORK.

1. On Bible-reader's Work: to continue the work of the Bible-reader's Association founded in 1868. (See Appendix 2.)

2. On Mothers' Meeting: to conduct meetings of women for sewing and reading, with religious exercises.

3. On Dorcas Work: to meet weekly and sew, for the purpose of supplying destitute Sunday-school children and others with clothing.

4. On Relief of the Poor: to distribute the poor fund of the Church, making annual report thereof directly to the Session.

5. On Tracts: to procure tracts and other religious reading, for distribution by the Visiting Committees and the Bible-reader.

6. On Pulaski Sunday-school Work: to care for the interests of the Pulaski Sunday-school, originated through this Society.

7. On Somerville Sunday-school Work: to care for the interests of the Somerville Sunday-school.

8. On Presbyterian Home: to aid the Presbyterian Home for Widows and Single Women, at West Philadelphia.

9. On Hospitals: to aid the Presbyterian and the Germantown Hospitals.

WORK WITHIN THE CONGREGATION.

1. On Systematic Visiting: to visit regularly all the families of the church and congregation.

2. On Social Receptions: to take charge of social meetings at the church.

3. On Providing Flowers for Church Services.

4. On Care of Church Building: to oversee the work of keeping it in order.

5. On Ladies' Prayer Meetings: to hold devotional meetings for the ladies of the congregation.

6. On Parish Library.

II.—ORDER OF EXERCISES.

The following order of exercises shall be observed at the regular meetings, viz.:

1. Reading of Scripture.
2. Silent Prayer.
3. Prayer and remarks by the Pastor, if present.
4. Reading minutes.
5. Reports from the Standing Committees in their order.
6. Unfinished business.
7. New business.
8. Adjournment.

At the annual meeting the following order shall be observed, after reading the minutes, and before taking up unfinished business:

1. Treasurer's annual report.

2. Appointment of Committee to nominate officers for the ensuing year.

3. Secretary's annual report.

4. Election of officers.

III.—FINES FOR ABSENCE.

Every member absent from a regular meeting, shall be fined ten cents, unless excused by the Executive Committee.

IV.—AMENDMENTS.

These By-laws may be amended, by consent of two-thirds of the members present at any meeting.

APPENDIX ADDED TO BY-LAWS IN 1870.

1. The Domestic Missionary Society was founded in 1852, for sending relief to needy missionaries under the care of the Presbyterian Board of Domestic Missions. During eight years, (1862 to 1870), it sent out nineteen boxes, valued at $4,500. The aggregate of its contribution to the cause, up to 1870, was not far from $10,000. In order to promote the efficiency of church work, it connected itself with the Pastoral Aid Society, May 4, 1870, taking the name and duties of Standing Committee on Domestic Missions.

2. The Bible-reader's Association was formed in 1868, for the purpose of carrying the gospel message to those who

are strangers to the sanctuary and its teachings, and also relief to pressing temporal wants. For this purpose a visitor is employed, and supplied with German and English tracts, and with funds for distribution. A Mothers' Meeting has been established in connection with it. One thousand dollars were received into its treasury up to May 4, 1870; at which date, in order to promote the efficiency of Church work, it connected itself with the Pastoral Aid Society, taking the name and duties of Standing Committee on Bible-reader's work.

[In order to present these methods of work in their true light, it may be well to mention that the above plan was formed as one part of a larger scheme, including the whole congregation. Most of the elements for organizing such a scheme have come into existence within the church, but it has always seemed best to act gradually, taking each step as the way for it was opened by the Providence of God, and therefore the final combination of these elements has not yet been made.

The idea was that of a Church League for Christian work, of which the Pastoral Aid Society would form the Ladies' Auxiliary, and a similar organization the Young Men's Auxiliary. The whole League would have for President, the Pastor: for Executive Committee, the Session; and for Financial Committee, the Board of Trustees. It would have a Sunday-school Section, another for Mission Schools, and one for each of the further objects which might be undertaken.

Any work which is best done by Young Men, or by Ladies, would be given to the proper Auxiliary: and that which requires the combined effort of both, to the League itself.

It would thus include all the active members of the church, and could very properly expect to have its various operations made the subject of prayer, exhortation, and discussion, at the second prayer meeting in each month : the first being given to Foreign Missions.

The existence of such a plan, even as an ideal not yet fully accomplished, has had its influence on the development of Church life, and is therefore mentioned in this place.]

www.ingramcontent.com/pod-product-compliance
Lightning Source LLC
Chambersburg PA
CBHW030545270326
41927CB00008B/1514